# BOLD
## *Leadership*

FOR ORGANIZATIONAL
ACCELERATION

**JIM TOMPKINS**

TOMPKINS
PRESS

Tompkins, James A.
    Bold leadership for organizational acceleration / Jim
Tompkins.
    p. cm.
    Includes bibliographical references and index.
    LCCN 2006911141
    ISBN-13: 978-0-9658659-9-9
    ISBN-10: 0-9658659-9-1


    1. Leadership.  2. Contracting out.  3. Success in
business.    I. Title.

HD57.7.T66 2007                      658.4
                          QBI07-600091

# Dedication

This book is dedicated to all the SPECIAL clients, friends, family and loved ones who have helped me understand the necessity of being **BOLD**.

Thank you.

Tim

# Acknowledgements

I would like to thank five groups of people for their support and insights. Without them, this book would not exist.

1. For their insights into inspirational leadership, I am much indebted to James Kouzes and Barry Posner. Their work, in particular their breakthrough book *The Leadership Challenge*, has had a major impact on my thinking.

2. For their support and thinking on outsourcing and core competency, I must acknowledge Steve Simonson, Bruce Tompkins and Brian Upchurch—my co-authors on the book *Logistics and Manufacturing Outsourcing: Harness Your Core Competencies*.

3. For their awesome support in every aspect of creating this book, I am grateful to Forsyth Alexander, Jerry Smith, Myra Schwartz and Cheyanne Ritz.

4. For his insights into resilience, I am most appreciative of the innovative concepts of Yossi Sheffi. In particular, I acknowledge his breakthrough book, *The Resilient Enterprise: Overcoming Vulnerability for Competitive Advantage*.

5. For allowing me to learn and practice implementing and refining the thoughts presented in this book, I thank the many clients of Tompkins Associates.

All the best,

## Jim Tompkins

James A. Tompkins, Ph.D.
CEO
Tompkins Associates
imtompkins@tompkinsinc.com

# Table of Contents

# Preface

I do not have a twin, but as you may have noticed, there are two of me. One of me, James A. Tompkins, Ph.D., writes books consistent with my supply chain/logistics education, thus using my Ph.D. handle.

The other one of me, Jim Tompkins, writes books based on my experiences. Well, this book is written by "both of me." Part of it is based on my technical expertise in core competency and outsourcing, and part of it is written based on my experiences in inspirational leadership and resilience. Therefore, consistent with my desire to not misuse my Ph.D. handle, *Bold Leadership for Organizational Acceleration* comes to you from Jim.

This book is written for the business executive. However, the *Bold Leadership* principles set forth in this book are equally applicable to people in all walks of life. To be successful in any endeavor in this day and time, one must be bold.

Written as a guide to becoming a bold leader, this book is applicable to anyone who wants to take control of his or her life and become more effective. The principles set forth within these pages will allow you to enhance your career and your life, to achieve more, and to be boldly successful.

# Part 1

*Inspirational
Leadership*

# Chapter 1
# BUSINESS ACCELERATION

---

"What you have been today isn't good enough for tomorrow."
  – Susan P. Peters, Vice President for Executive Development, G.E.

---

## "Faster, faster!"

What was once a shout on the swings from the playgrounds of our childhoods now echoes the demands of our customers. For a business or enterprise to succeed today, speed—not time—is of the essence. In 2000, Bill Gates wrote, "The 21st century will be about velocity: the speed of business and the speed of change."[1] Time has proven that Bill Gates was right.

Beginning with the fall of the Berlin Wall almost 20 years ago and bolstered by the advent of technological advances, Internet connectivity and instant messaging, the world has morphed into a global village where almost anyone can connect with another person in another part of the world at any time. You, your son, or your daughter can easily be chatting on an instant messaging program with a co-worker in Australia while writing an email to a cousin in England and using a program to have a free voice conversation with a friend in Peru—all at 8 p.m. on a Saturday night. We are all linked now and information is instantaneous. Who would have predicted that *Time Magazine*'s 2006 Person of the Year would be, of all people, You! And how did "You and I" rise to this honor? We helped create the success story of "community and collaboration on a scale never seen before" with the World Wide Web as our tool in our business and personal lives.[2]

At the same time, there are more countries in the world producing a greater amount of goods; this has resulted in a marketplace that is broken into smaller segments. All of these phenomena are creating the demand for speed in every aspect of the organization. Business acceleration is a way of life today, not some prediction for the future.

---

[1] Bill Gates, *Business @ the Speed of Thought: Succeeding in the Digital Economy.* (New York, NY: 2000), pp. i.

[2] Lev Grossman, "Time's Person of the Year: You," *TIME Magazine*, 13 Dec. 2006, http://www.time.com/time/magazine/article/0,9171,1569514,00.html?aid=434&from=o&to= http%3A//www.time.com/time/magazine/article/0%2C9171%2C1569514%2C00.html

# BOLD LEADERSHIP for Organizational Acceleration

## Speed and More Speed

We demand speed everywhere, grinding our teeth when we're put on hold and told that our wait time will be five minutes or beating our steering wheels when we have to wait at a stoplight. There's "speed dating" and its equivalent in procurement, "speed matching." A popular monthly magazine, *Fast Company*, is devoted to helping companies compete and expand in this era of acceleration. The world's largest computer manufacturers are introducing servers with faster processors because we crave more speed. They are also offering systems designed to guarantee no business disruption should a server or two fail or a natural disaster shut down a server room, because the few minutes that servers are taken down for maintenance are a few minutes too long.

The Internet and the Web have helped create this sense of urgency. We use both tools to start and foster dialogues and relationships, resolve differences between systems and platforms, and learn more about individual customers. Enterprise application integrators (EAIs), enterprise service buses (ESBs), and web application servers tie disparate systems and programs together. Auto ID, wireless communications technology, and business software have been standardized, and system integrators have written custom interfaces to allow the exchange of data between programs.

All of these developments have made the notion of immediate orders a reality, and we all want our products to arrive almost as soon as we've ordered them. A frequent comment from Tompkins Associates clients is, "People click, and they expect the order's shipping time to be just as quick." It's not just customers who want their products as soon as possible. Marketing departments also want to get a new product launch completed and get rid of inventory before it becomes obsolete. Executives want their companies to grow as quickly as possible.

Global connectivity allows us to work 24 hours a day, continuously racing our competitors to be the "first to market," the "first to customer," the "first to the capital markets." New trade agreements, individual countries partnering with each other to produce and export goods, international e-commerce, and web applications have created a 24/7, on-demand, global marketplace and supply chains that mirror it. This point is driven home by Thomas Friedman in *The World Is Flat: A Brief History of the Twenty-First Century*. He describes his meeting in Bangalore with a top engineer from Infosys in which the engineer tells him a great truth: The enormous investment in establishing broadband connectivity worldwide during the 1990s, the corresponding explosion of software development that included segmenting development in modules that could travel, and lower prices for computers made it possible for developers to work remotely. When the engineer added that this had leveled the playing field, Friedman has a revelation: "The world is flat…. Clearly it is now possible for more people than ever to collaborate and compete in real-time with more people on more different kinds of work from nore different corners of the planet and on a more equal footing than at any previous ime in the history of the world—using computers, e-mail, networks, teleconferencing, nd dynamic new software."[3]

Politics and technology took us down this path, but the current focus on reducing costs and increasing profits has cemented it into a requirement for doing business today. On 26 February 2004, Jeffrey R. Immelt, Chairman of GE, speaking in front of a group of investors, had this to say about globalization: "Globalization has a bad name. But the world is inextricably global."[4] Immelt is right. There's no going back now. If customers can get products faster and cheaper because they're being manufactured in China while they sleep, by workers who accept lower pay, then those are the products they are going to buy.

Friedman agrees, although he states that globalization has been around since 1492, when Columbus set out for the West Indies. He says that there are actually three eras of globalization. The first, Globalization 1.0, began in 1492 and lasted until 1800. During that time, countries explored the possibilities of muscle power, horsepower, wind power, and steam power and in so doing, began a march toward global integration. Globalization 2.0 began about 1800 and lasted until 2000. This era, fueled by faster transportation, the telephone, electricity, fiber optic cabling, and the early days of the Internet and World Wide Web, created multinational companies, successfully shrinking the size of the world "from medium to small."

In 2000, he says, the world entered Globalization 3.0, which differs from the first two eras because not only is the world flattened, but the individual, rather than the company, now has the power to collaborate and compete globally. The driving force is not horsepower and not hardware, but software applications that have "made us all next-door neighbors."[5]

There are arguments over whether these developments are good or bad. Friedman sees them as a good thing; others find them frightening.[6] No matter how you look at it, though, one thing is true: In this, the Globalization 3.0 era, it takes much more effort to establish a brand and this increases the importance of providing quality service. At the same time—after more than a decade of de-layering, reengineering, downsizing, and deverticalizing in efforts to improve efficiency and reduce cost base—companies are smaller.

---

Thomas L. Friedman, *The World is Flat: A Brief History of the Twenty-First Century.* (New York: 2005), pp. 6–7.

"Immelt's Big Cheer for Globalization," *BusinessWeek Online*, 27 Feb. 2004, http://www.businessweek.com/bwdaily/dnflash/feb2004/nf20040227_2342_db039.htm

Friedman, *The World Is Flat*, pp. 9–11.

"Editorial: A Deeper Look at the Flat World," Oxford Leadership Academy, September 2005. http://www.oxfordleadership.com/Articles/articles_main.asp?aid=32; "The World is Flat: A Brief History of the Twenty-First Century." Book review. *Interface*. May 2005, http://bcis.pacificu.edu/journal/2005/05/friedman.php

# Sowing Seeds in Chaos: Google

Google, not even a decade old, is worth about $125 billion and reports that it makes $10 billion a year in revenue. What is the secret of such phenomenal success when other giants like Ford and Viacom are struggling? Google attributes it to a management model that is founded on the wish of co-founders Larry Page and Sergey Brin that Google not be like any other company.

For example, recently a Google vice president made a mistake to the tune of several million dollars. When she went to Larry Page's office and apologized, saying that she made the mistake because she moved too quickly and had no controls in place, Page surprised her. After thanking her for her apology, he said "I'm so glad you made this mistake. Because I want to run a company where we are moving too quickly and doing too much, not being too cautious and doing too little. If we don't have any of these mistakes, we're just not taking enough risk."

Google's senior vice president of operations, Shona Brown, argued in a 1998 book that anarchy in a company isn't always a bad thing—and that is why Page, co-founder Sergey Brin, and CEO Eric Schmidt hired her in 2003. The way to succeed in today's fast-paced

*Continues on next page*

The result is that everyone in business organizations has too much to do and not enough time to do it. CEOs are pressed, but so too are those who hold entry-level positions. The notion of "24/7" is now "28/9," even though that isn't possible. Company leaders are given 15 pounds of apples and told to fit them into 5-pound plastic bags. The reality is that we have much more work to accomplish in our quest to achieve customer satisfaction, grow business, and increase profitability and we have almost no time to do it. Our business climate today is best characterized as chaotic, and most companies have no real sense of how to handle it.

## Handling the Apples

How are company leaders answering this call for speed? Well, as I see it, they're doing one of three things with their apples. Some are watching their apples spill out of the bag. They've heard the call for speed, but they've decided that they can't do anything about it. They're kicking the apples out of the way, tossing away the bag (either on the ground or into the hands of another company) and giving up. They close their businesses and find some other way to make a living.

Others keep stuffing the bag as if they have only 5 pounds of apples, even though they know that the bag won't hold them all. They close their eyes and keep shoving them down, hoping that by sheer force, the apples will fit. In other words, they continue to try to conduct business the old way—concentrating too much on the physical aspects of expansion or allowing functions that are not core competencies to eat up most of their precious time. These apple-weary folks are hoping that today's business challenges are hurdles that can be conquered by pushing them down.

Unfortunately, a 5-pound bag can't hold 15 pounds of apples, no matter how much stuffing you do. So, the bag breaks and apples go everywhere. Their companies rupture and their leaders are left with very little to salvage. Some even end up in re-structuring programs. These companies are suffering because they continue to do business as if it were still the early 1990s.

No one is immune. The number of companies admitting that their business models do not work anymore is increasing. Recently, Ford and Viacom admitted that they need to change the way they do business or they will not make money, and even Dell and pharmaceutical giants Merck, Pfizer, and Bristol-Myers Squibb say that they must develop new ways of doing business. The pressure is on and company boards and other stakeholders are not patient—if you do not fix things in a short period, you are toast.[7] In some ways, it's almost better to be like the company that gives up, because they haven't expended all their energy trying to get ahead by doing the same things they've always done.

The third possible response to the puzzle is to look at the apples and the bag and rely on innovation to develop a way to get those apples in the bag without breaking it. Some are sorting the apples, keeping the ones that look the best, and giving the rest away. Others are making applesauce, putting it into the bag, and then sending the bag to someone to put in jars. Another group is taking seeds from the apples and using them to plant new trees. Some are making applesauce and using the seeds to plant new trees. These are the companies that are thriving in the current business climate through bold leadership.

## The Good News: There Is Hope

An increasing number of company leaders are either facing ruptured bags or the threat that they might break. These leaders can take heart, however, because there is hope. The leaders that have made applesauce are not all that different from them—some may even have gotten the idea to make applesauce when the first few apples got smashed on the ground. A good example is Lou Gerstner of IBM. When he took over IBM in 1993, the company was on the brink of disaster. The company had lost sight

chaos, she says, is to try not to create too much structure while not having too little either. "If I ever come into the office and feel comfortable, if I don't feel a little nervous about some crazy stuff people are doing, then we've taken it too far," she adds.

Crazy is definitely the norm at Google. The company's meetings usually start on the hour, and young employees will congregate outside scarce conference rooms before the meetings, doodling on hallway whiteboards and sharing private, inside jokes about expanding the company's online advertising campaign. The company figures out things as it goes, using helter-skelter spending and a "spaghetti" method of development, which is described as "toss against wall and see if it sticks," and requiring all engineers to spend 20% of their time pursuing their own ideas. In 2006, Google surprised the business world when it acquired YouTube, the popular video sharing website. Eric Schmidt of Google said that the acquisition was about vision, not about business, and that the YouTube guys reminded him of the early days of Google. Analysts even said the acquisition was crazy. However, the purchase is an example of how Google operates. One technical analyst has described it like this: "Get the right people on the bus and then they'll figure out where to drive it."[8]

*Continues on next page*

[7] Geoffrey Colvin, "Managing in Chaos." *Fortune*, 2 Oct. 2006, pp. 79–82.

Although it has made some mistakes, Google has made even more money—generating about $800 million each quarter. Since it went public in 2004, its stock value has increased more than four times the original starting price—from $85 a share to $400.[b] Crazy? Maybe. Successful? Definitely.

---

[a] Anders Bylund, "Google buys YouTube," *Arstechnica*, 9 Oct. 2006, http://arstechnica.com/news.ars/post/20061009-7942.html. "Google buys YouTube: GooTube," *Boing Boing*, 9 Oct. 2006, http://www.boingboing.net/2006/10/09/google_buys_youtube_.html.

[b] Adam Lashinsky, "Chaos by Design: The Inside Story of Disorder, Disarray, and Uncertainty at Google and Why It's All Part of the Plan," *Fortune*, 2 Oct. 2006, pp. 86–98.

of its customers and was completely mired in its arrogant, top-down, "it's our way or the highway," mindset, and this was killing it. But, in only nine years, he transformed the company and brought it back from the brink. It took a lot of hard work and Gerstner had to make unpopular decisions, but in the end, he saved the company.

Arrogant mindsets are being phased out, as many successful leaders are creating new ways to manage and motivate. The incredibly fast-paced, information-packed environment we live in has caused a shift in leadership style. A leader can misspeak, and the comment can be instantly reported to a worldwide audience through blogs, text messages, television and other mass media outlets. Because of scenarios like this, integrity and vision are more important than ever.

Leaders must adapt to the intense pace of a society that is linked together in this way. Instead of just telling others what to do, leaders listen more, discuss their vision and participate in the management and motivation of people. Executive coach and author Marshall Goldsmith describes it this way: "The great achiever: It's about me. The great leader: It's about them."[8]

So, the good news is that there is success to be had in this era of organizational acceleration. Those leaders that are trying to survive by doing business the way that they have always done can become the next Meg Whitman of eBay or Jeffrey Immelt if they leave the status quo behind. Great leadership always involves a change in the status quo and a willingness to take risks, and both of these company leaders have kept their organizations in the forefront of success by constantly seeking ways to build on their successes, yet not being afraid to shed a familiar piece of the business if necessary.

For example, Whitman has successfully overcome strong competition from Amazon.com and Yahoo!. She ad-

---

[8] "Today's leaders juggle e-mails, blogs and integrity," CNN.com, 8 Jan. 2007, http://www.cnn.com/2007/US/01/07/pysk.overview/index.html

dresses and solves problems quickly and works to weed out fraudulent items and offers on her site. As a result, eBay has posted a consistent flow of profits, making it the world's most valuable Internet brand. Whitman does not rest on her laurels; instead, she continuously seeks to add services and improve the eBay experience. Recently, she negotiated the acquisition of Skype Technologies, a company that offers high-quality voice communications to anyone with an Internet connection anywhere in the world. This acquisition was met with curiosity; some analysts questioned the reasons for it.[9]

Those familiar with Whitman and the Skype product, however, have recognized the ingeniousness of the purchase. The Skype software is easy to download and install and enables free calls between Skype users online. After it is integrated with eBay, Skype is expected to streamline and improve communications between eBay buyers and sellers because buyers will be able to talk to sellers in real time, thereby quickly getting the information they need to buy. Sellers will have a faster method for building relationships and closing sales. As a result, Skype can increase the velocity of trade on eBay, especially in categories that require more involved communications such as used cars, business and industrial equipment, and high-end collectibles. With this acquisition, Whitman has recognized that speedier service is essential for eBay.

As for Immelt, many wondered if he would be able to fill the gigantic shoes left by Jack Welch, who, for years, has been hailed as *the* corporate leader to emulate. Immelt has startled the world by not trying to be Welch, but instead turning GE into an innovator, full of new ideas and channels. Immelt has definitely grasped the concept that a company will not be successful in the early decades of the 21st century if it maintains the status quo. His goal is to spur growth far above the company's current 4 percent growth rate without losing their productivity edge. He had devised a six-part growth model, and company leaders are not only charged with applying initiatives to it but also are using it to explain new initiatives.[10] In addition, he has sold divisions of GE that have not been very profitable (such as insurance) and pared down slower-growth, small-margin divisions like small appliances. At the same time, GE has acquired businesses that allow the company to establish itself in such hot areas as cable and film (Universal Studios, Telemundo, and Bravo), biosciences (Amersham), and security (Edward Systems).[11]

But that's just the tip of the iceberg. Immelt believes that the best way to achieve sustained organic growth is through innovation. One of the first things he did when he took over in 2001 was invest $1 billion in research and development.[12] Immelt has also

---

[9] David Kirkpatrick, "Why Skype? EBay's Still Thinking Big," *Fortune*, 12 Sept. 2005, http://www.fortune.com/fortune/fastforward/0,15704,1103966,00.html

[10] Thomas A. Stewart, "Growth as a Process," *Harvard Business Review*, June 2006, pp. 60–70.

[11] "The Immelt Revolution," *Businessweek*, 28 March 2005, http://www.businessweek.com/pdf/250332BWEPrint.pdf

[12] Stewart, Growth, pp. 60–70.

## The Importance of Company Values: Sam Palmisano

When Sam Palmisano took over as the CEO of IBM in 2002, IBM had come through one of the most difficult periods in the company's history. Lou Gerstner had guided it through that time and transformed the company from a mainframe maker to a hardware, software, and network solution provider. Palmisano's task was to continue IBM's transformation, but he instinctively knew that to do that, he could not continue on Gerstner's path. Instead, the long-time IBMer decided that it was time for the company to reexamine its values.

To do this, he decided to conduct an experiment that many (since that time) believed to be more innovative and daring than some of the products being developed in IBM labs. In July 2003, he used the IBM intranet to host "ValuesJam," a three-day online discussion with approximately 50,000 IBM employees where he asked them to discuss IBM's values. The first 24 hours were difficult because many employees used that time to share opinions that many IBM executives did not want to hear. One participant went so far as to say, "The only value in IBM today is the stock price." But when the executives urged Palmisano to shut down ValuesJam, he refused.

The result was that after three days, the responses became more positive and at the end, the

*Continues on next page*

instigated "Imagination Breakthrough" requirements for the company's leaders—each must submit at least three proposals to a council Immelt established that will change GE's direction or alter its brand image or perception in the public eye.[13] He has also restructured the way products are made for countries other than the U.S. He decided that taking a product and removing features for countries outside the U.S. wasn't working. The result of that decision was the formation of a team of 25 people to change the philosophy from removing features to learning what customers in other countries needed and building products for them. So far, these changes have been very successful; in October 2005, GE announced that its third-quarter earnings would meet the high end of earlier projections.[14]

The lesson to be learned from Whitman and Immelt, along with other movers and shakers like Jeff Bezos of Amazon.com, Bill Gates (love him or hate him, he is still a visionary), Michael Dell, Sam Palmisano of IBM (see sidebar), the triumvirate at Google (Eric Schmidt, Larry Page, and Sergey Brin) and more, is this: Leaders must not only be bold if they want to thrive today, but they must also develop bold companies—encouraging boldness in all aspects of the organization.

### Becoming Bold

Exactly what does it take to be bold? In the 30 years that I have been helping clients, I have been pondering the answer to this question. At first, I thought that extraordinary leadership was the answer. But, once I started examining the concept of leadership, I realized that being a bold leader is not enough. A bold company also requires boldness in every level of the organization, from management to support staff. Leaders must therefore teach others how to be leaders. Their strategies must be flexible and innova-

---

[13] "The Immelt Revolution."

[14] Greg Levine, "Faces in the News: Google Eyes Semel's Yahoo! Library; Jobs' Apple Event: Video IPod?; Trump Lauds Tough Ladies," *Forbes.com*, 7 Oct. 2005, http://www.forbes.com/2005/10/07/video-ipod-trump-cx_gl_1007faceweek.html

ive. They must challenge the established view of a leader s someone who leads and demonstrate that leadership neans inspiring others to lead. They must have the cour- ge and spirit to move from wherever they are to further heir abilities to lead others into getting extraordinary hings done. In other words, these leaders must practice nspirational Leadership. And this is why I have devoted he next four chapters to this most essential type of lead- rship that fuels boldness throughout all organizations.

Having courage and spirit, which is at the heart f being an inspirational leader, is important. This is ecause bold and inspirational leaders must understand nd help others understand that the company will have to nake significant changes to the way it is doing business o that it can grow and thrive in an accelerated business nvironment. This means looking at the big picture and searching for the parts of that picture that are just filling p canvas and not adding value to the subject.

Actually, it is not enough just to look at the big icture. If your picture is in a frame, you need to look at he frame too. Is it possible that the frame is the impor- ant part and the picture inside it needs to be changed or emoved? In other words, are you better at supporting he products your company makes than making them? Or is the frame that holds the picture rotting or overpower- ing the picture so that it is totally lost? That is often the case—CEOs and other company leaders are spending so much time repairing the parts of their companies which support their core competencies that they have lost sight of the competencies themselves. Basically, companies must critically examine themselves and determine what their core competencies are. They must also make sure they are concentrating their energies on the actions that will bring them success in their core competencies. To do this, everyone must understand their companies' goals and have contributed to putting a strategic vision and plan in place.

company had enough information, which they mined using one of their own programs, to create a revised set of values: "Dedication to every client's success," "Innovation that matters—for our company and the world," and "Trust and personal responsibility in relationships." These were shared with employees.

Palmisano then acted on the new values and gave the director of his e-business unit and his 15 direct reports the task of identifying the gaps between the values and company practices. The company overhauled almost all of the ways they did business, even going as far as selling the PC division to the Chinese computer manufacturer Lenovo, changing the way it priced items by offering a price for services that not only provide hardware but also the integration and support to run them, and working in partnership with a major shipping line to develop Radio Frequency Identification (RFID) tags that will identify shipping containers and help track them from place to place. These days, IBM is going strong and company employees are more excited about working there. When Palmisano is asked if values really matter, he can prove to them that they do.[c]

[c] Paul Hemp and Thomas Stewart, "Leading Change When Business Is Good," *Harvard Business Review*, 1 Dec. 2004, pp. 61–71.

After the core competencies have been identified, they can be subdivided into primary and secondary cores. This is analogous to separating the apples to put in the bag from those to keep out of the bag. Bold leaders and companies can then take steps to make sure that leaders and managers are concentrating the right amount of their precious time on those core competencies by letting others handle everything else. If leaders do this, then the company has a much greater chance of success. So many organizations have failed because not enough executive time was spent handling core competencies and executives were bogged down in the minutiae of physical expansion or antiquated IT systems that required constant maintenance and expenditures. When those worries are removed from the company leader's shoulders, the leader is free to focus on what is really important.

Of course, once you have identified core competencies, then it is time to look to other companies outside your organization to do the work that you have decided takes too much time away from focusing on your core. In other words, you must have an outsourcing plan and you must find organizations that have the experience to help you make your plan a reality. This is somewhat related to identifying core competencies, but it goes well beyond. There is no way, in this day and age, that companies can do it all. Outsourcing has taken on unnecessary negative connotations fed by analysts who say we're going to lose all our jobs to India, Mexico, and China. But in reality, outsourcing is the smart thing to do. If your company has decided to expand into a new market as part of its bold program, then it makes sense to seek out others who may know that market and work with them to ensure that your expansion is a success.

Not long ago, I would have told you that if you had a company that practices inspirational leadership and has taken the time to identify core competencies and outsource, then that company has an excellent chance of thriving in today's business climate. However, recent events such as 9/11, the Asian Tsunami, Hurricane Katrina and other disasters—combined with the increasingly complex yet fragile supply chains that have been created to support globalization—have led me to realize that being bold also means elevating business resiliency from contingency planning to a critical business strategy. If you do not know what will happen to your company after a natural disaster, a major power outage or even a terrorist attack, then your company does not have much of a chance of surviving should something like that occur. Your company must know exactly what it will do to recover from a disaster. Moreover, it is not enough to just know what your company will do; to be bold, you must also know what your supply chain partners and outsourcing providers will do.

"The supply chain is getting leaner, with less buffer and more inventory being held in other countries," observed Steve Phillips, CIO, Avnet Inc., a distributor of electronic components and computers, in a recent *IndustryWeek* interview. "This means there is less ability for the supply chain to soak up the shocks that occur."[15] To counteract this, a bold organization invests in technology and relationships that provide them with visibility into the whereabouts of parts and materials shipments, as well as the critical paperwork that must accompany them.

So to be bold, a company must excel at three things: inspirational leadership, core competency and business resilience. The purpose of this book is to show you how to create inspirational leaders, how to determine your core competency or competencies, and understand what it takes to be a resilient business. When you have them all down and recognize that you must never stop growing or evolving, then you will truly be **BOLD**.

*****

*If you were on an elevator with a colleague and had something important to explain, you would have to do it quickly and eloquently. These "On the Elevator" sections at the end of each chapter in this book work the same way. They are quick, succinct summaries for you to use on-the-go. The last chapter is a summary of the book in this format.*

## On the Elevator

Organizational acceleration is affecting all of us. Customers want our products and they want them now. However, downsizing, reengineering, re-layering and deverticalization have created smaller companies with fewer employees. Therefore, there is no longer enough time in the day, week, or even year for us to get everything done quickly.

Leaders travel one of three paths when faced with this acceleration. Some give up and close their company doors, taking a job elsewhere. Others keep trying to do business the way they have always done it and as a result, they will lose marketshare and customers because you can no longer be all things to all people today. The third path is to reexamine every aspect of the organization, and with a combination of innovation and boldness, redirect the company so that it can meet customer demands.

To thrive in this climate, companies and their leaders must be bold. To be bold takes:
• Inspirational leadership
• A combination of core competency identification and strategic, innovative outsourcing
• A business resiliency strategy

This book explores each of these attributes, starting with inspirational leadership, then moving to core competency and business resilience.

---

[15] Doug Bartholomew, "Supply Chains At Risk," *IndustryWeek*, 1 Oct. 2006, http://www.industryweek.com/ReadArticle.aspx?ArticleID=12713

# Chapter 2

# INTRODUCTION TO INSPIRATIONAL LEADERSHIP

"Leadership and learning are indispensable to each other."
– John F. Kennedy

Today's organizations cannot conduct business as they did 10 or 20 years ago and neither can their leaders. As stated in Chapter 1, developments in the late 20th and early 21st centuries have changed the rules of business forever. These developments have also created the following new realities:

- Globalization—Political events have led to the formation of a global village with virtual links between all of its inhabitants.
- Computer power—There is more computer power in my car than there was in the first manned space flight. A video camera has more power than the IBM 360, and my own personal computer has more power than actually existed in 1950.
- Connectivity—Thanks to innovations like the World Wide Web and networks, we are all linked. Information is instant.
- Fragmentation—Yes, globalization, computer power, and connectivity have linked us all together. But at the same time, countries are producing more goods and services, and this has broken the marketplace into smaller segments.
- Knowledge—Knowledge has replaced capital. Nowadays, companies must focus on knowledge-adds rather than value-adds.
- Social contract—More people are entering the realm of self-employment and establishing virtual commitments instead of "live" business interactions. The result is that loyalty has shifted from business to individuals.
- Search for meaning—These days, there is a yearning for a greater purpose. Books on values, virtues, and spirituality are all bestsellers.

These realities have redefined the meaning of success. And to meet the challenges created by the above realities, the place to be professionally is in a bold organization that encourages collective and individual growth. However, an organization cannot be bold without inspirational leadership. It is inspirational leadership that drives an organization into boldness and, ultimately, into sustainable success.

What is inspirational leadership? The answer to this question is not simple. It is often best explained as a combination of characteristics that gives people the courage and spirit to move from wherever they are and further their abilities to lead others so that they can get extraordinary things done and make a difference.

Inspirational leadership is more than being a leader—it is about inspiring others to lead with a combination of heart, deeds, learning, and being rather than doing. In this chapter, I introduce you to inspirational leadership—first by addressing some of the myths about leaders in general and examining two popular misconceptions about leadership, and then explaining what it is.

## Myths about Leaders

For the past couple of decades, we have been hearing and reading stories about specific company leaders—for example, Bill Gates, Michael Dell, or Martha Stewart—and what has gotten them to the top. As a result, we have formed ideas of what these leaders are like based only on their publicity (good and bad). Over time, these images get sharper and sharper as more people discuss and write about these high-profile leaders, and suddenly they are accepted as truths. As a result, the following statements about leaders are fairly common and are often accepted as fact:

- Leaders create organizations that run like clockwork.
- Leaders are renegades who do things differently from the rest of us.
- Leaders are interested in immediate results and not the long term.
- Leaders can predict the future.
- Leaders are machines that process and analyze spreadsheets.
- Leaders are compelling and fascinating people who can charm just about anyone into doing just about anything.
- Leaders are into command and control.
- It's lonely at the top.
- Leaders must lead from ivory towers.
- Only a few can lead.

In reality, these statements are myths. You need to dispel them as you open your mind to inspirational leadership. So, let's take a closer look at each one.

***Leaders create organizations that run like clockwork.*** This implies an organization where all the cogs and wheels are in place and turning at just the right time. The problem with this idea is simple—no organization runs like clockwork. A leader who tries to make it run this way is not an inspirational leader. He is simply a person who winds the clock (or changes the battery). If the key is lost, or a cog gets knocked out of place, or the battery is not in stock, the clock winder is ill-equipped to deal with the situation. This is not a bold organization! It is one that tries to conduct business as usual in a world where business is no longer usual. (See Chapter 1.) Bold organizations are full of challenges and changes—they are all about shaking things up so that each challenge becomes an opportunity and change is embraced.

*Leaders are renegades who do things differently from others.* Merriam Webster's Online Dictionary defines a *renegade* as: "1. a deserter from one faith, cause, or allegiance to another. 2. An individual who rejects lawful or conventional behavior."[16] *The American Heritage Dictionary* adds, "An outlaw; a rebel."[17] We tend to romanticize renegades by concentrating on their implied rebellious and unconventional behavior. However, these definitions suggest at best someone who is wishy-washy and at worse, a traitor. Think about it: Is a person who fits these descriptions going to be good for an organization? No. They are more likely to leave the organization in the midst of a crisis, perhaps to go work for a competitor. Also, the key to inspirational leadership is to attract constituents and inspire them to be leaders. Someone with an outlaw personality, steeped in defiance, cannot do this. The outlaw might attract constituents, but he or she is incapable of inspiring or fulfilling them.

*Leaders are interested in immediate results and not the long term.* It has been suggested that we are living in a world populated by people with very short attention spans. Some experts refer to this as "pseudo ADHD." Therefore, there is a tendency to revere leaders who turn a bad situation around quickly or initiate a sale or plan that generates a great deal of revenue in a short amount of time. It's a form of instant gratification in a world that has increasingly shifted its notion of long-term from 5 years to 6 months. The problem is that turning a situation around quickly or taking steps to create a noticeable spike in revenues for a quarter or two can hurt the company in the long run. A good leader can set short-term goals, but these goals should also contribute to a long-term plan that assures that the company will be netting benefits far into the future.

*Leaders can predict the future.* The idea that leaders can see into the future is a very popular one. The people who believe this idea like to cite the group of company founders and CEOs that have prospered from the rise of the personal computer and the Internet/World Wide Web as examples of those who can predict the future. They claim that this group saw into the future far enough to realize that they would profit from technological developments. Actually, what they don't realize is that these leaders didn't see into the future—they shaped it. Real leaders have no better handle on the future than their employees—what they do instead is direct their energies toward inspiring others to create their futures.

---

16  http://www.m-w.com/dictionary/renegade
17  http://dictionary.reference.com/search?q=renegade

# The Myths of CEOs

In November 2005, *Inc.* magazine published its list of America's 500 fastest growing private companies. One of their writers, Keith McFarland, decided to see if certain myths about entrepreneurs held true: They thrive on risk; they are poor strategists; and they are bullies.

McFarland administered the Test of Attention and Interpersonal Style, a personality exam used by the public and private sector, to 250 former and current leaders of the *Inc.* 500. The results were surprising:

- Thriving on risk: The test indicated that although fast growth CEOs enjoy facing adversity, they are more likely to manage and mitigate risks than take them.
- Poor strategists: The test indicated that the *Inc.* 500 CEOs actually see the world as problems to be solved and tend to think strategically. They scored in the 92nd percentile on the ability to think strategically.
- Bullies: Rather than showing that the *Inc.* 500 CEOs force others to do their bidding by unpleasant means, the test indicated that these CEOs succeed by helping other people—employees, partners, investors, and suppliers—become successful themselves. The CEOs scored higher than 82 percent of the population on their ability to express

*Continues on next page*

*Leaders are like machines that process and analyze spreadsheets.* People often think that good leaders have few emotions other than a devotion to the bottom line. They point out that the leaders of companies like General Motors, G.E., and IBM review, interpret, and analyze spreadsheets and then make cold decisions to lay off thousands of workers, while the media hail them for turning their companies around. The truth is, however, that you cannot be an inspirational leader if you are detached or aloof. Inspirational leaders have feelings—plenty of them—and that's a good thing. To inspire others to perform extraordinary feats, you need to be passionate and have intense enthusiasm and positive emotions.

*Leaders are compelling and fascinating people who can charm just about anyone into doing just about anything.* Leaders, especially politicians, often have charisma. Something about them charms people and makes them sit up, take notice, and follow their lead. But a leader does not have to be charismatic to inspire others. All it takes is a strong belief. In fact, a strong belief relayed passionately is far more likely to encourage others than surface charm or a hypnotic personality. Beliefs are things that others can hang onto, whereas charisma has no substance.

*Leaders are into command and control.* The military uses command and control techniques to keep soldiers in line on and off the battlefield. This helps countries win wars. However, despite some claims to the contrary, an organization is not a battlefield and employees are not soldiers. There is little room for command and control in a bold organization populated by inspirational leaders and inspired employees. A command and control mentality does not leave any room for personal growth and development. In fact, the more you try to control employees the less likely they are to excel. Leaders must serve and support.

*It's lonely at the top.* If a leader is lonely, then it is likely that he or she is operating with the command and control mentality. Loneliness is caused by isolating yourself from others, either physically or mentally. If you spend your time in your office, reviewing revenue and earnings charts, making decisions based on them, and ordering others to carry them out, all without connecting with those around you, then you are not an inspirational leader. Your employees will characterize you as someone who is out of touch and does not understand them or their needs. These feelings breed unrest and discontent—hardly a recipe for success. To be an inspirational leader, you must be involved and in touch with those who work for you.

***Leaders lead from ivory towers.*** This notion is related to the idea that a leader must be at the top of the organization or on a higher plane than the rest of the organization. Neither is true. You might be at the top of the company's organizational chart, but that's as far as you should go in relating leadership to a place. Leadership is a process, not a place. An inspirational leader must be fluid, moving throughout an organization to view all levels. I will discuss this topic again later in this chapter.

***Only a few can lead.*** In some ways, I think that this is the most dangerous myth perpetuated in business today. It encourages people to give up by giving them an out. If you believe that there can only be a few leaders in the world, then you have a manufactured excuse for failure. You simply say, "Only a few can really lead—look at Bill Gates and I'm no Bill Gates. You can't expect me to be a leader." My answer to this is simple. Think about what might have happened if Bill Gates had said, "I'm no Ray Dolby," or "I'm no J. Paul Getty." The fact of the matter is this: Leadership is everyone's business. We all have leadership potential—inspirational leaders help us dig down deep and bring the inner leader out into the light. By encouraging others to lead, inspirational leaders also create leaders who turn around and inspire yet another group. In the end, there are numerous leaders. Maybe there are a few people out there who can't lead, but I've yet to meet any.

support and encouragement. This was higher than any other group except high performing salespeople.[d]

---

[d] Keith McFarland, "The Psychology of Success," *Inc.*, November 2005, pp. 158-160.

# Leadership is Who You Are, Not What You Do: Self Appraisal Questions

To help you understand the difference between who you are and what you do, I have developed the following self-appraisal:

- Are you okay with yourself?
- Are you okay with others?
- Is there something you're worried about?
- Is there something you know you should do but you have avoided?
- Is there someone you can help?
- Is there someone you can make feel good about themselves?
- Are your priorities okay today?

Think about your answers carefully. Being okay with yourself means that you have self-acceptance and self-confidence. If you are okay with others, there will be no shadows preventing you from leading. If you're not okay with others, find out why and work to dissipate those shadows.

If you're worried about something, identify it and remove it. This will remove another shadow from yourself. If there is something you haven't done that you know you should, go ahead and get it out. This will allow you to be true to who you are.

Ask yourself who you can help and how. Then, do it. This builds who you are and defines you. Now, find people that you can

*Continues on next page*

## The Two Things It is Not

Much has been written on the subject of leadership. In fact, if you do a search on Amazon.com for leadership books, the result is a list of more than 174,000 titles.[18] If you read the introductions to these books, you find all kinds of theories about what leadership is or what one must do to be a good leader. Rarely do they tell you what leadership is NOT. However, to help you gain a true understanding of inspirational leadership, it is important for you to know what it is NOT about. There are two popular misconceptions about leadership that can color your perceptions. I would like to clear these up.

The first misconception is that inspirational leadership is a position. We often hear people talk about being in a leadership position—as if leadership were a place. Position, or place, implies being in a fixed location, unable to move beyond a certain point. Can you imagine a leader that doesn't move? How effective could that leader be?

Leadership, the kind that is the heart of inspirational leadership, cannot be restricted in this manner. Inspirational leaders are dynamic. They move and they grow. They are constantly learning. Most importantly, they are constantly encouraging others to learn and grow as well. You cannot do this if you're stuck in one place.

Given that notion, you might be tempted to think that inspirational leadership is based on actions and results. After all, you've probably heard this statement on numerous occasions: "Leaders act." Of course, a leader must act and get results, but the fact is that this is the second misconception that can derail the process of becoming an inspirational leader. This is because inspirational leadership is not about what a leader does, but instead, it is about who the leader is. It is a matter of where you focus your mind. In other words, inspirational leaders concentrate on being rather than doing. The result is a solid list of positive attributes that guide individuals and organizations.

---

[18] Search of amazon.com for "Leadership" in "Books" conducted 10 Nov. 2005.

When you focus only on output and deliverables, you lose sight of the big picture and you become bogged down, tired and irritable with no impetus to guide, inspire, or grow. Table 1 demonstrates the different attributes associated with being and doing. As you can see, the attributes for each are a world apart.

| Being | Doing |
|---|---|
| Content | Output |
| Relationships | Busy |
| Substance | Activities |
| United | Self-centered |
| Peaceful | Hectic |
| Considerate | Harsh |
| Patient | Anxious |
| Enthusiastic | Task oriented |
| Recognize others | Find faults |
| Confident | Calculating |
| Generous | Selfish |
| Others first | Me, me, me |

TABLE 1. BEING VERSUS DOING.

In summary, inspirational leadership is not a place, and it is not a "to do" list. So, it's best to stop thinking of leadership as anything but a dynamic, mobile force. At the same time, you must not focus on what you are doing as a leader, but rather on your whole being—inspirational leadership is a state of mind that will lead you to inspire others to accomplish the extraordinary. Now that you know which misconceptions you must shed in your quest to become an inspirational leader, you are ready to consider the answers to two questions: What is inspirational leadership about, and what does it require?

## What Is It All About?

Inspirational leadership is about tapping the wellsprings of human motivation and about fundamental relationships with humanity. It is also about setting examples by deeds rather than by words. Inspirational leadership means being a role model and not a general who relies on words, speeches, and memos. It means you demonstrate rather than remonstrate.

make feel good about themselves and determine how to do it. This further defines you.

By examining your priorities today, you can see who you are. If they are not okay, then reorganize them and put them in order. This is leadership.

In simpler terms, inspirational leadership is about the human heart and those things we associate with it. As I mentioned earlier, the myths about leadership imply that leaders should approach activities objectively, not subjectively. The problem with being objective is that with it comes an inability to inspire and motivate others to act as leaders, because there is nothing behind objectivity except facts. To be an inspirational leader, you must be subjective, because the cornerstones of inspirational leadership are human characteristics and attitudes, and not facts. These cornerstones are:

- *Relationships* (people)—Building relationships with people so that they will be inspired and empowered to learn and do extraordinary things.
- *Emotion* (feelings)—Inspirational leadership is not possible without the emotions and passion to motivate others.
- *Caring* (concern)—This means demonstrating genuine concern and caring about people and ideas; otherwise, they will feel you are talking the talk and not walking the walk.
- *Joy* (true celebration)—Taking the time to celebrate small and large victories joyfully is a big part of inspirational leadership, because it inspires confidence and makes others look forward to the next victory.
- *Sharing* (genuine)—Honest, bilateral give and take is a big part of inspirational leadership. If you are secretive and don't share important events and ideas, no one will want to share them with you.

Inspirational leadership is also about learning. That's right—inspirational leaders are learners. Not only are they learners, but they also learn to be leaders by leading. What is even more interesting is they learn it best by leading in the face of obstacles. Just as weather shapes mountains, so do problems shape leaders. Think about the last time someone solved a problem for you. Do you remember how that person solved it? Most likely you do not. You might remember the solution, but even if the person explained how they got to the solution, you probably don't remember what they said.

Now, think about the last time you solved a problem. Do you remember how you and your team solved it? Most likely you do. So, if you are presented with both the problem you solved and the problem someone else solved again, you are most likely to be able to handle the one for which you developed the solution. We all learn the most in difficult times.

Inspirational leaders then take the lessons they learn and use them to teach others to learn during adversity. Therefore, in a sense, inspirational leaders live their lives backwards. They see in their minds' eyes what the results look like even before they start a project, much as designers create layouts or drawings before an installation. They can do this because they take the projects that came before and use the lessons learned from them to shape the current project.

## What Does It Require?

Inspirational leadership is an acquired skill. You are not born with it. Instead, it is something you learn, and that means it can also be taught. At the same time, you cannot learn inspirational leadership by sitting on the sidelines. You can only learn it by doing—by trying new ideas and gaining knowledge from those ideas that pan out and those that fail. As you find things that work, you add them to your secrets of success. To create your team of inspirational leaders, you need to give them the opportunities to discover their own secrets of success. As you and your leaders acquire these secrets of success, you also grow. This growth allows you and your leaders to evolve to fully understanding inspirational leadership, and thus becoming inspired leaders.

Inspirational leadership also requires constituents. There are numerous definitions of constituent, most of them related to politics. In this context, constituents can be thought of as supporters, much as constituents support representatives in politics. Constituents support their leaders and, much like politicians must woo the electorate, inspirational leadership requires winning constituents. To do this, leaders must understand them, speak their language, and present a compelling case for becoming constituents. You do not command constituents—you enlist them and then inspire them.

The final main requirement for inspirational leadership is dialogue. To enlist constituents and to meet the sharing cornerstone of inspirational leadership, you must listen. No monologues are permitted. When you speak to others, ask questions and then listen so they feel that you care. They will open up to you and in doing so, you are much more likely to win their support. Once you have won support, then you have added to the constituency that is so vital to inspirational leadership, and you are ready to take on the five fundamental practices of exemplary leadership. These practices are the subject of the next chapter.

## On the Elevator

To meet the business challenges created by today's new realities, the place to be professionally is in a bold organization that encourages collective and individual growth. However, an organization cannot be bold without inspirational leadership. It is inspirational leadership that drives an organization into boldness and, ultimately, into sustainable success.

Inspirational leadership is a combination of characteristics that give people the courage and spirit to move from wherever they are to further their abilities to lead others to get extraordinary things done, and to make a difference. Inspirational leadership is more than being a leader—it is about inspiring others to lead with a combination of heart, deeds, learning, and being rather than doing.

To open your mind to inspirational leadership, you must clear your mind of the following myths:

- Leaders create organizations that run like clockwork.
- Leaders are renegades who do things differently from the rest of us.
- Leaders are interested in immediate results and not the long term.
- Leaders can predict the future.
- Leaders are machines that process and analyze spreadsheets.
- Leaders are compelling and fascinating people who can charm just about anyone into doing just about anything.
- Leaders are into command and control.
- It's lonely at the top.
- Leaders must lead from ivory towers.
- Only a few can lead.

You must also abandon the two main misconceptions about leadership: that inspirational leadership is a position and that leadership is based on what you do.

Inspirational leadership is about tapping the wellspring of human motivation and about fundamental relationships with humanity. It is also about setting examples by deeds rather than by words and about learning while leading, especially in the face of obstacles.

Inspirational leadership requires planning, executing, managing, and controlling. It also requires constituents, or supporters, who must be enlisted and not commanded. Enlistment comes from dialogue and not monologue. Listen to learn.

# Chapter 3
# FUNDAMENTAL PRACTICES OF
# INSPIRATIONAL LEADERSHIP

"Exciting things can happen during a crisis and you can improve your business by taking the lessons learned and making adjustments to the way your business operates."

A bold organization must have inspirational leadership. In Chapter 2, I introduced inspirational leadership and described it as a combination of characteristics which gives people the courage and spirit to move from wherever they are and further their abilities to lead others so that they can get extraordinary things done and make a difference. I also discussed the myths of leadership and listed the attributes you need to develop to become an inspirational leader. Then, I stressed the importance of enlisting constituents, which is critical. You cannot grow to be an inspirational leader or create inspirational leaders without constituents.

The good news is that you don't have to "wing it" because I am sharing the secrets of inspirational leadership through these fundamental practices:
- Challenge the process
- Inspire a shared vision
- Enable others to act
- Model the way
- Encourage the heart

Each practice, of course, requires certain commitments. In this chapter, I explain these practices and describe their commitments.

## Challenge the Process

Challenging the process is a fundamental practice of inspirational leadership— being a bold organization means changing the status quo. As I mentioned earlier, your organization cannot be bold and will not succeed in today's marketplace if it maintains the status quo. Therefore, inspirational leaders cannot afford to operate with a "business as usual mentality." Instead, they must be willing to step out and take risks.

## Steve Jobs— Opportunity from Crisis

On June 12, 2005, Steve Jobs, the CEO of Apple and Pixar Studios, gave the commencement address at Stanford University. In this address, he told a story he said was about "love and loss." Jobs described how he turned a personal crisis into an opportunity. Ten years after Jobs founded Apple, he was fired by his own company. For a few months, he foundered and was publicly branded a failure. Then, he came to an important realization: "I still loved what I did. The turn of events at Apple had not changed that one bit. I had been rejected, but I was still in love. And so I decided to start over."

During the five years that followed his firing, he started two companies, NeXT and Pixar: "Pixar went on to create the world's first computer animated feature film, *Toy Story*, and is now the most successful animation studio in the world," he said. "In a remarkable turn of events, Apple bought NeXT, I returned to Apple, and the technology we developed at NeXT is at the heart of Apple's current renaissance." The renaissance that Jobs spoke of includes the development of the iPod, a product that has revolutionized the way we listen to music and watch movies.

In his story about love and loss, Jobs also said, "I didn't see

*Continues on next page*

To challenge the process, make the first two commitments of inspirational leadership:

1. Seek opportunities for change, growth, innovation, and improvement.
2. Experiment by taking risks and learning from your mistakes.

Let's take a closer look at these commitments.

### Commitment #1—Seek

Business has always been difficult, and it has become even more so in the last decade. As I see it, business leaders today have two choices: maintain the status quo and figuratively wring their hands while the business crumbles or take advantage of the good things that this decade has brought and use them to their advantage. A useful analogy is one I used in *Revolution: Take Charge Strategies for Business Success*, that of the dinosaur and the crocodile. Dinosaurs represent the leaders and businesses that maintain the status quo: They were once quite powerful, but now they're extinct because they could not adapt to a changing world. Crocodiles actually existed before the dinosaurs and still exist today because they know how to adapt to new circumstances. They are comfortable with growth and change, and they are driven by stretching, pushing, pulling, and improving.[19]

Making commitment #1 involves a fundamental change in the way you view crises and challenges. Instead of viewing them as negatives that cause problems and headaches, view them in a positive way as events that can take your organization to new heights. In other words, view each problem not as an obstacle to overcome but as an opportunity for growth, innovation, and success.

Think about the last crisis in your organization. During that time, it is likely that you accomplished what you once thought was impossible. This is because when a crisis surfaces, rules, habits, procedures, standards and norms are

---

[19] Jim Tompkins, *Revolution: Take Charge Strategies for Business Success.* (Raleigh, N.C.: 1998), pp. 40.

put aside. It shines a light on a situation and provides you the opportunity to realize that exciting things can happen during a crisis and that you can improve your business by taking the lessons learned and making adjustments to the way your business operates.

It is important to stress that you should not wait for a crisis or problem to make commitment #1. Inspirational leaders cannot be passive, sitting around and waiting for an external issue to create an opportunity; they must be active. They must stay on top of the exciting developments in technology and business and use them to define new paths or directions for their organizations. That is part of being innovative.

### Commitment #2—Experiment

Challenging processes is not for the faint of heart. You must have the courage to experiment with new ideas, new products, new structures, and so on. This is because true innovation does not come about the first time out. Rarely does someone "get it right the first time." You must take risks and learn from your mistakes. As I mentioned in Chapter 2, inspirational leadership is about learning and that includes the lessons created from mistakes, both monumental failures and small "gotchas."

An example of commitment to learning from the mistakes you make when you experiment is a form of computer programming called "Extreme Programming" or "XP." XP is based on innovation through failure, because the goal is to write a unit test that proves a certain piece of code will break so that, eventually, almost flawless code is created. In fact, one of the five values of XP is "courage."

Wikipedia briefly describes the courage value of XP: "Courage enables developers to feel comfortable with refactoring when necessary. This means reviewing the existing system and modifying it so that future changes can be implemented more easily. Another example of courage is knowing when to throw code away. Every pro-

it then, but it turned out that getting fired from Apple was the best thing that could have ever happened to me. The heaviness of being successful was replaced by the lightness of being a beginner again, less sure about everything. It freed me to enter one of the most creative periods of my life."[e]

---

[e] "'You've got to find what you love,' Jobs says," *Stanford Report*, 14 June 2005, http://news-service.stanford.edu/news/2005/june15/jobs-061505.html

grammer has experienced getting stuck on a complex problem in their own design and code after working on it all day, then coming back the next day with a clear and fresh view and rapidly solving the problem in half an hour."[20]

Commitment #2 requires taking the principles that extreme programmers use in their programming and applying them globally. Inspirational leadership means being comfortable with refactoring business when it is warranted. And the best way to refactor business is to try new practices and principles and see what happens. Some of them will work and some won't. Keep the ones that work and learn from the ones that don't by noting why they didn't work, so that you don't attempt them again.

### Inspire a Shared Vision

It's a "no brainer" that inspiring a shared vision is a fundamental practice of inspirational leadership—since inspiration has to be at the heart of it all. To act on this practice, imagine a better future for your company. Think big and think positively. The sky is the limit. Once you have done that, you can't keep it a secret. You need to communicate this future enthusiastically and passionately with your constituents until they share not only your vision of the future, but also your enthusiasm and passion. So next, make the third and fourth commitments:

3. **Envision** an uplifting and enabling future.
4. **Enlist** others in a common vision by appealing to their values, interests, hopes, and dreams.

### *Commitment #3—Envision*

Think back to your childhood. You had goals and dreams of your future then and you daydreamed about them for hours. These aspirations had a powerful impact on your life and functioned as your vision of future success. You can do the same thing for your company by envisioning an uplifting and enabling future.

You can start by asking yourself where your company is headed and how it will get there. Now, think of the science of your business and if that fits your vision. If it does, then great. If it does not fit, then think about how the science of your business might change. And even further—you can think about the values you want practiced and how you plan to measure success. Then ask yourself if the vision is doable and if it is, think in high-level terms of how it could be achieved.

Unlike your childhood daydreams, however, this is not an exercise that can be accomplished with a few random thoughts. Take some time to think about your vision of the future. This is important. Your vision can start as a "pie in the sky" statement but

---

[20]  http://en.wikipedia.org/wiki/Extreme_programming

eventually, you must come down to earth and think of all the ingredients in the pie. You must also be prepared to put ingredients in the pie that others will think are delicious. Others must want the pie as well, and this is the fourth commitment.

### *Commitment #4—Enlist*

It is going to take more than just yourself to make your vision a reality. You can't do this alone. If you try, you will fail. So, you need to enlist others (such as your constituents) in your vision until you all share it. You are the champion of this vision, but you must also sell and promote it. You can breathe life into it and make it exciting and fun.

The best way to inspire a shared vision is to know your constituents. Learn as much about them as you can—who they are, what they do, what they love, what they hate, where they want to go, and where they don't want to go. Once you know them, you can appeal to their values, interests, hopes and dreams. It is possible that you might need to make some minor adjustments to your vision to enlist your constituents, but this is a good thing. By making your vision appeal to more than just yourself, you are truly sharing it.

## Enable Others to Act

Leaders use the word "We" to include others. It's been my experience that relinquishing control is one of the most difficult things for people, including many leaders, to do. However, you cannot be an inspirational leader of a bold organization without the help of your constituents. That is why enabling others to act is one of the fundamental practices of inspirational leadership. To enable, you must make the fifth and sixth commitments:

5. **Foster** collaboration by promoting cooperative goals and building trust.
6. **Strengthen** people by giving power away, providing choices, developing competence, assigning critical tasks, and offering visible support.

### *Commitment #5—Foster*

When people band together to accomplish goals, there is greater manpower, greater intelligence, more resources, more talents, and more diversity. The strength gained by working with others who share your vision is almost immeasurable. Inspirational leaders should always, therefore, open the doors to their dreams to other people and allow them to act. They should use whatever means they have at their disposal, including team-building and organizing for success, to promote cooperative goals and build trust.

I have found that exercising three basic rules of behavior with constituents goes a long way toward facilitating trust, participation and cooperation:

- Total honesty: Encourage your constituents to say what they think. Let them know they can express their views and contribute to the business, but make sure that there are no politics, no games-playing, and no adversarial relationships.
- Total amnesty: Assure your constituents there will be no repercussions when they express their goals and their thoughts. Then stick to your word.
- Listen to others: One of the best ways to build trust and cooperation is to listen. Make eye contact, minimize distractions, and paraphrase (in your own words) what the speaker has just told you. If your constituents think that you're listening and digesting what they say, they will not only trust you, but they will learn to listen themselves. Soon there will be trust everywhere.

### *Commitment #6—Strengthen*

Inspirational leaders strengthen by building, developing and increasing the power of others. To do this, they must give power away, which is another reason why inspirational leaders do not lead with a "command and control" mentality. As I stated earlier, one of the most difficult things for people to do is "let go." At the same time, it is one of the best things you can do as a leader. By letting go of the reins and having others take them up on your behalf, you are strengthening your leadership position and your business.

Like collaboration, this strengthening process is a science. You should not apply it haphazardly. Instead, work to strengthen judiciously. Also, never abandon your constituents even as you give them more power. Instead, you should:

- Offer them choices. Don't force your constituents to come up with solutions and ideas alone. Encourage them to apply critical thinking skills by providing a series of solutions and letting them decide what they believe is the optimum option.
- Develop competence. Encourage your constituents to learn and grow, and make sure that you let them learn from their mistakes. Just as you become an inspirational leader by learning from your mistakes, so do your constituents.
- Assign critical tasks. An excellent way to strengthen others and build their trust is to give them important and essential jobs to accomplish. When a person finishes a project or assignment that is key to the success of a business, the pride of accomplishment creates confidence and makes a person stronger.
- Offer visible support. One of the mistakes companies made in the 1990s was to adopt the word "empowerment" and use it as an excuse to abandon their employees to the wolves. Just about everyone in the world wants to hear that they are on the right track or that they are close to the right track. At the same time, they want to know that someone else is there to provide aid if they stumble. Inspirational leaders do not abandon their constituents; their doors are always open to them.

# Chapter 3: FUNDAMENTAL PRACTICES OF INSPIRATIONAL LEADERSHIP

## Model the Way

There is an old joke that goes: "Do as I say, not as I do." This is exactly what an inspirational leader must avoid. Instead, act the way you would want your constituents to act. You must model the way and carry out the seventh and eighth commitments of inspirational leadership:

7. **Set the example** by behaving in ways that are consistent with shared values.

8. **Achieve** small wins that promote consistent progress and build commitment.

## *Commitment #7—Set the Example*

After you have enlisted others to share your vision, which includes goals and values, you must demonstrate your commitment by acting. Again, you want others to do as you do. You must inspire them with your behavior, much like a role model. We all know that people are inspired by other people and how important role models are to civilization. Well, this is your chance. You can be a role model to a group of people through your deeds and your words.

For example, if a value that your constituents have decided to share is honest communication, then you yourself must communicate honestly. Share your stories. You cannot be close-mouthed or hide your feelings and expect others to turn around and communicate honestly with you.

Consider another example: If you tell your constituents that your door is always open to them, then make sure that the door stays open and that you are there. There is nothing more frustrating than knocking on a door that you have been told is always open only to find that most of the time, it is either closed or no one is behind it. When you keep the doors open, you will find your constituents will soon keep their doors open too.

## *Commitment #8—Achieve*

Achieving small wins will promote consistent progress and build commitment. In other words, the best way for you to both share and accomplish your vision is to set goals that build on each other until your vision is real. This is not unlike the prescription for tackling any project—from organizing your household to establishing a new company. Divide the project into smaller, "doable" tasks that can be accomplished in a short period. In this way, you set your pace. You can then count each completion of the task "a win" that spurs you on to the next task. Before you know it, your project is complete, and you have not been overwhelmed by it. Instead, you have pride in a job well done.

Moreover, if you give your constituents finite goals to accomplish in a reasonable amount of time to help make your shared vision happen, then they will soon feel a certain amount of ownership in the vision. The more "wins" they experience, the more committed they will become. They will also see progress and feel positive and enthusiastic.

# Creative Celebration: Lands' End

Lands' End, the clothing and merchandise retailer based in Wisconsin, uses creative celebration to acknowledge the accomplishments of their employees. Here are a few of their 2004 activities:

- They picked a theme for the year and aligned it with the 2004 Olympics, calling it "Going for the Gold." They used that theme throughout the year in company meetings and for celebrations and recognition.
- On September 29, 2004, employees and their families, retirees, community members, and local students joined Lands' End for the "World's Largest Pillow Fight." After the pillow fight, they made a donation of pillows and pillowcases (valued at almost $100,000) to charity. The pillowcases were embroidered with "Sweet Dreams from Lands' End." "Maintaining Lands' End as a great place to work is important—whether it's through giving back to the community, creating a fun work environment, or delivering quality products and service to our customers," said Mindy Meads, the firm's CEO in 2004. "Hosting an event like this was an excellent way for us to have some fun, make history, and support a good cause."

*Continues on next page*

## Encourage the Heart

I have heard that business and heart do not mix. This corresponds with the leadership myth noted in Chapter 2 that leaders are like machines that see spreadsheets and not people. Inspirational leaders know that heart is an integral part of all bold organizations. Encouraging the heart by building self-esteem is critical to being an inspirational leader. To encourage the heart, move to the ninth and tenth commitments:

9. **Recognize** individual contributions to the success of every project.

10. **Celebrate** team accomplishments regularly.

### *Commitment #9—Recognize*

Inspirational leaders understand the immense power of recognition. The need for emotional support and emotional recognition is a part of every person and requires constant attention. Think of football and basketball coaches—they do not sit quietly on the sidelines waiting for the game to be over to provide feedback. They are involved with the game and give emotional support and recognition for each and every play.

Inspirational leaders are like coaches. They write notes of appreciation, verbally recognize employees in public and private, and use certificates, plaques or other tangible items to demonstrate not only achievement but also their genuine appreciation for the work done by individuals and teams. Key ways that inspirational leaders recognize others include:

- Continually provide positive reinforcement to acknowledge achievements, especially the "small wins" mentioned previously.
- Allow spontaneity and genuine excitement for shared visions, goals, and values to surface.
- Make a regular habit of saying "Thank you."
- Provide specific recognition in real-time mode.
- Recognize both individuals and teams for great performance.

• Be aware of and sensitive to the feelings of the person or team being recognized, as well as the feelings of others.
• Always recognize first in private and then in public.
• Be consistent and genuine in the recognition process.
• Be natural, allow others to be themselves, and have fun while providing recognition.

## Commitment #10—Celebrate

In today's corporate world, there seems to be more criticism than recognition. If someone does a wonderful job, it's accepted silently. But if a mistake is made, that person is sure to hear about it. At one time, such criticisms were given in private; but these days, as the stress of being a 24/7 or even, impossibly, a 28/9 world takes its toll, these criticisms often become public. This is difficult for everyone—people care about how others perceive them.

Inspirational leaders of bold organizations realize that public criticism harms the business and the company. However, they also recognize the power of public reinforcement. Each time a person, a team, or the whole company achieves a win or accomplishes a significant goal, there should be a celebration. When one person or a team has gone above and beyond the call of duty to contribute to the success, inspirational leaders create celebrations not only to honor those responsible for the achievement, but to let everyone know that achieving a goal aligned with a mission is worthy of a celebration as well.

Some leaders prefer to hold regular celebrations and others prefer to hold spontaneous ones. An inspirational leader combines the best of both–a regular celebration that underscores monthly or quarterly progress and spontaneous celebrations for major accomplishments. In this way, their constituents know that the celebrations are special and meaningful, and their desire to pursue the shared vision is strengthened.

• Lands' End hosted a Summer Olympics from July 13 to August 21, which featured such events as marshmallow golf, a beach ball throw, the plank walk, a free throw contest, and the gurney push. The top five teams at each event were awarded points and the top team for each event was awarded a traveling trophy, and "celebrity" status. The event also included opening and closing ceremonies, and all finalists were honored at the company picnic.

• "Torches" were sent to various departments in the company. The division that could most creatively display their torch received extra credit towards the Lands' End Olympics. Each department found a unique location, displayed the torch, captured the moment, and submitted a photo. The company intranet displayed the various locations where the torch traveled. The mighty torch ended up in Rome, Japan, in the Lands' End swimming pool, on the roof, on a tractor, and many more places.[¹]

---

[¹] Bob Nelson, "It's a celebration," *Bizwomen.com*, 25 July 2005, http://www.bizjournals.com/bizwomen/consultants/return_on_people/2005/07/25/column322.html

## What's Next?

This chapter has discussed the fundamental practices of inspirational leadership and the commitments that must be made as part of these practices. You have learned what you need to do to enlist others in your visions and dreams and about the processes involved in becoming a leader. The important thing to remember is to learn by doing and that each triumph and failure is part of the process of becoming an inspirational leader.

Now that you have the playbook, it's time for you to learn more about your teams (your constituents) and their expectations of you. This is addressed in the next chapter.

## On the Elevator

The good news about inspirational leadership is that you don't have to "wing it." It involves achievable, fundamental practices:

- Challenge the process: Challenging the process is a fundamental practice of inspirational leadership because being a bold organization means changing the status quo.
- Inspire a shared vision: To act on this practice, imagine a better future for your company. Think big and think positively. Once you have done that, you can't keep it a secret. You need to communicate this future with your constituents enthusiastically and passionately, until they share not only your vision of the future but also your enthusiasm and passion.
- Enable others to act: Leaders use the word "We" to include others. You cannot be an inspirational leader of a bold organization without the help of your constituents.
- Model the way: To be an inspirational leader, you must act the way you want your constituents to act. You must show them your commitment to your shared vision, goals, and values.
- Encourage the heart: Inspirational leaders know that heart is an integral part of a bold organization. Encouraging the heart by building self-esteem is critical to being an inspirational leader.

Each of these practices requires certain commitments:

1. Seek opportunities for change, growth, innovation, and improvement. This is part of the Challenge the Process practice.
2. Experiment by taking risks and learning from your mistakes. This is part of the Challenge the Process practice.
3. Envision an uplifting and enabling future. This is part of the Inspire a Shared Vision practice.
4. Enlist others in a common vision by appealing to their values, interests, hopes, and dreams. This is part of the Inspire a Shared Vision practice.
5. Foster collaboration by promoting cooperative goals and building trust. This is part of the Enable Others to Act practice.

6. Strengthen people by giving power away, providing choices, developing competence, assigning critical tasks, and offering visible support. This is part of the Enable Others to Act practice.
7. Set the example by behaving in ways that are consistent with shared values. This is part of the Model the Way practice.
8. Achieve small wins that promote consistent progress and build commitment. This is part of the Model the Way practice.
9. Recognize individual contributions to the success of every project. This is part of the Encourage the Heart practice.
10. Celebrate team accomplishments regularly. This is part of the Encourage the Heart practice.

# Chapter 4
# FOLLOWING THE LEADER

Napoleon said, "A leader is a dealer in hope." Constituents want their leaders to be forward-looking and focused on a positive future for their team members.

A bold organization is fueled by inspirational leadership. Leaders must challenge the process, inspire a shared vision, enable others to act, model the way, and encourage the heart. However, it is also important to understand that inspirational leadership is a reciprocal process between those who choose to lead and those who choose to follow. Simply put, you cannot lead in a vacuum; leadership requires constituents. To understand leadership, you must fully grasp the constituent/leader relationship. Successful leaders care about their people. In this chapter, I discuss the expectations that constituents have for their leaders.

## What Constituents Expect

One of the best ways to demonstrate that you care about your constituents and what they think is to put yourself in their shoes and think about their expectations. You can do this by remembering what it's like to be a constituent and what characteristics you like in your own leaders. For this, I propose a simple exercise.

In Table 1, there are 20 characteristics that constituents seek in leaders. Look them over and then rank your Top 4, with 1 being the most important.

| Ambitious | Caring | Honest | Loyal |
| Broad-minded | Dependable | Inspiring | Mature |
| Competent | Determined | Intelligent | Self-controlled |
| Courageous | Forward-looking | Imaginative | Straightforward |
| Cooperative | Fair-minded | Independent | Supportive |

TABLE 1. LEADERSHIP CHARACTERISTICS.

Now that you have given this some thought, compare your answers with the rankings in Table 2, which shows the results of this exercise (part of a study conducted by James Kouzes and Barry Z. Posner in 1987.[21])

| | | | |
|---|---|---|---|
| Ambitious—16 | Caring—13 | Honest—1 | Loyal—19 |
| Broad-minded—7 | Dependable—11 | Inspiring—4 | Mature—15 |
| Competent—2 | Determined—17 | Intelligent—5 | Self-controlled—18 |
| Courageous—12 | Forward-looking—3 | Imaginative—9 | Straightforward—8 |
| Cooperative—14 | Fair-minded—6 | Independent—20 | Supportive—10 |

TABLE 2. LEADERSHIP CHARACTERISTICS—RANKED.

As you can see, the Top 4 characteristics are: honest (#1), competent (#2), forward-looking (#3), and inspiring (#4). Interestingly, when Kouzes and Posner conducted another study in the 1990s, the Top 4 characteristics did not change. Honesty was still Number 1, but the other three shifted such that forward-looking was second, inspiring was third, and competent was fourth. However, I like to present these characteristics in the order of the 1987 studies and that is what I have done here.

### #1 Being Honest

Honesty is the most important characteristic people look for in their leaders. Constituents want their leaders to tell the truth and they want their leaders to act consistently with their stated values and principles. They observe leaders to see if they are going to "walk the talk" and if they do what they say they will do. They want to be treated fairly and within the values the leaders have articulated.

It really is no surprise that honesty is the characteristic most constituents consistently look for in a leader. After all, we want to be sure that the person we follow is worthy of our trust. Constituents want to be led by someone who is truthful, ethical, and principled. They want to be confident of that person's integrity. As a result, they associate the following words with honesty:

- *Trust:* Constituents want to be able to trust their leaders. Trust is achieved by honest leaders because of the consistency between their words and deeds.
- *Truthful:* Constituents equate being honest with being truthful. Again, they are looking for behavior that validates words.
- *Standards:* Constituents expect leaders to have standards. In that way, they know where you stand.
- *Principled:* Constituents want leaders with principles. They expect them to be willing to take a stand and to have confidence in their own beliefs.

---

[21] James M. Kouzes and Barry Z. Posner, *The Leadership Challenge*, 3rd Ed. (San Francisco: 2003.)

- *Values:* Constituents expect leaders to have values. They feel that leaders with the right values will be more honest.
- *Ethics:* Constituents believe that being ethical is related to being honest. Even though you can be honest without being ethical, the honesty they seek includes ethics.

As these words indicate, constituents measure honesty not by what we say, but by hat we do. They measure honesty by behavior, because they want to see honesty and ot just hear it. They judge honesty based on whether we are practicing what we preach.

The real key here is being honest with yourself. When you're honest with yourself, ou can identify your strengths and expand on them. This is where you make your mark, dd your greatest contributions, and leave a legacy. We all do our best work when we re honest with ourselves, because this gives us the energy and confidence to lead and ach others.

The other key is to demonstrate integrity. As Stephen Covey said, "Integrity cludes but goes beyond honesty. Honesty is telling the truth—conforming our words reality. Integrity is conforming reality to our words—keeping promises and fulfill- g expectations."[22] In other words, you must be consistent in both thoughts and deeds. you make a commitment, you must keep it. If you set goals, you must meet them. herefore, you must be sensitive to what you say and commit to, so there is no discon- ect between what you say and do. And whatever you do, you must communicate with our constituents—straightforwardly and openly.

## 2 Being Competent

Leaders must be capable and effective. Constituents want to follow someone with record of achievements. Therefore, the person who leads must be competent to lead. t the same time, leaders do not need to know everything that their constituents know. emember, the question isn't whether you are highly competent, but whether your onstituents perceive you to be. The two are connected, but the emphasis should be on e perceptions of your constituents. The characteristics that constituents are seeking in lation to being competent are:

- *Capable:* Recent leadership research shows that leaders need to demonstrate that they are capable. Constituents expect them to have skills related to the nature of their business. This is contrary to the popular business thought of the past 20 years that an "outsider," someone from another business entirely, can be an effective leader. Actually, trends have shown that such "outsiders" are viewed as not under- standing or not having the skills needed to lead.

---

Covey, Stephen, *The Seven Habits of Highly Effective People.* (New York: 1989.)

## Ethical Business Practices: Seth Goldman and Honest Tea

In 1999, Honest Tea CEO Seth Goldman produced the world's first organic tea, but there were only a few distributors who carried his products. One of those distributors was Whole Foods, who tasted the tea during a presentation and immediately ordered 15,000 bottles. "Now, a few years later, his Bethesda-based company, Honest Tea, is selling to Canada Dry, the Smithsonian Institute, an airline, and other high-profile organizations."[8]

"With revenue of $6.5 million, Goldman's company has made *Inc.* magazine's list of the 500 fastest-growing companies twice and has earned national recognition from the Natural Foods Industries for Socially Responsible Leadership, the American Vegetarian Association and other food industry groups."[9]

He has proven that a food product can be sold without sweetening it up, without taxing the environment and without hurting the little guy. Goldman's teas carry the Fair Trade logo, meaning workers in the tea gardens must make minimum wage or better. He has used his company to provide jobs in depressed areas, including a Native American reservation with 67 percent unemployment. And, of course, the organic product is

Continues on next page

- *The ability to ask good questions:* If you demonstrate that you are thoughtful by asking questions which demonstrate your knowledge and understanding of the mechanics of your business, constituents will be more likely to perceive you as being competent.
- *Achievements:* Constituents are looking for a track record of performance. They expect leaders to demonstrate competence at achieving their vision.
- *Winning track record:* People usually judge leaders by their results. You need to demonstrate that you have experience getting results. If you aren't achieving the goals and getting the results you promised, you won't have willing followers for long.
- *Leadership skills:* Constituents expect their leaders to be capable of leading. This ties into achievements and winning track records—they want their leaders to have demonstrated leadership abilities.

Interestingly, research has shown that leaders do not have to demonstrate competence in every aspect of their business. Usually, if leaders demonstrate competency based on the characteristics above, they can be perceived as competent. Also, while constituents expect leaders to show technical competence (knowledge of the mechanics of their chosen business), it is important to understand that technical competence does not necessarily refer to the leaders' abilities in the core technology of the operation. In fact, the competence that constituents demand varies by position and organizational condition.

It is also important to understand that until you master the leadership competencies that are important to your organization in the 90th percentile, constituents will not really notice them and thus they will not have a meaningful effect. If, for example, you are seen as someone who focuses on results at a level of 70 percent and you work hard for a year so that your rating goes up to 80 percent, this increase will not result in your being seen as an "excellent" leader. It is only when you truly excel in a competency that people

otice and draw favorable inferences from it. (The same
true in reverse for low scores; you are only viewed as
competent when you dip below 10 percent.)

Therefore, striving leaders who only dabble at a
competency and increase their skill marginally over the
course of a year are really wasting their time. You must
commit yourself to boosting your skill to the 90 percent
level so that your constituents perceive you as being both
an excellent leader and a highly competent one.

The good news here is that competencies are for the
most part learned and learnable. All it takes is motivation
and the desire to be effective. If you have both, tackling a
competency or competencies is not difficult.

## 3: Being Forward Looking

Napoleon said, "A leader is a dealer in hope."
Constituents want their leaders to be forward-looking and
focused on a positive future for their team members. They
expect their leader to be the "magnetic north" that provides others with the capacity to chart their course toward
the future. They see a forward-looking leader as having:

- *A vision:* It is not enough to simply have a vision.
  To be perceived as forward-looking, a leader must
  understand the vision, have experience forming and
  pursuing a vision, and know the power of a vision.
- *A dream:* Everyone has a dream. However, leaders
  who are viewed as forward-looking by their constituents are ones who can share their dream and
  invite others to contribute to it.
- *A goal:* In the section on competence, I stated that
  constituents want someone to demonstrate the ability to achieve goals. However, for constituents to
  believe that you are forward-looking, you need to
  communicate the goals clearly.
- *Planning abilities:* Constituents will not perceive
  you as forward-looking unless you can demonstrate
  that you can plan. You must show that you can plan
  as well as dream, envision, and set goals.

made without using pesticides or herbicides.[

"The first thing we did was in 1999 when we brought out the first fully organic bottled tea. We brought it out in partnership with the Crow Indians of Montana. We buy the peppermint from them and we give a portion of our sales back to their community," Goldman stated in an interview with the *Baltimore Sun* in 2002. "Then in 2001, we brought out a product called Community Green that involves a partnership with City Year, a national community service nonprofit, a sort of urban Peace Corps program. Then this year we introduced this product called Haarlem Honeybush, which is fully organic. It's a tea that we source from this small community in South Africa. We take it, put it in a bottle and sell it. Part of our sales royalty goes back to them.

"We are trying to show employers that they can be profitable without ignoring the impact of their decisions on their customers, the ecosystem and on working conditions of the poor," added Goldman.[

ᵏ "Growing Big But Staying Honest," *Maryland Daily Record*, 2004, http://www.mddailyrecord.com/innovator/2004honesttea.html

ʰ "Growing Big But Staying Honest."

ⁱ "Growing Big But Staying Honest."

ʲ "Honest Tea's Best Policies," *Baltimore Sun*, 5 Aug. 2002, http://www.baltimoresun.com/community/guide/bal-goldman080502,0,7403309.htmlstory?coll=bal-relocation-features

- *Strategy:* Strategy is related to planning in the minds of constituents. They want you to be able to indicate the steps that you will take together to put your plan into action. However, it is important that you not dictate these steps, but instead share them and invite changes or additions.
- *Capability to chart the course:* Imagine that you are the captain of a ship. How long do you think you can remain the captain if you cannot steer the ship to its destination? Before long, you would have mutiny on your hands. Think of your business as a ship. If you are able to set the direction of that business and your organization and steer it toward your goal, your constituents will see you as forward-looking.

A vision, a dream, a calling, a goal—you can call it what you like, but whatever it is it is clear that before constituents sign up that they want to know where they are heading. In other words, you must know where you are going if you expect others to willingly follow you on the journey. When you ask constituents about where their company is headed, many will respond, "I don't know, but I hope it is better." Now, more than ever, it is a leader's job to engage the full potential of the workforce by communicating possible outcomes.

Of course, you must also be dedicated to execution. But at the same time, remember to always share your forward-looking views and most importantly, your passion about future possibilities. Your constituents want you to have a sense of direction, a concern for the future, and the ability to set or select a desirable destination. Therefore, you must engage your constituents in the pursuit of greatness, not the avoidance of failure. Use words to paint a vivid, rich picture of what the future will look like, feel like, and be like.

## #4 Being Inspiring

In Chapter 3, we explored the fundamental leadership practice of inspiring a shared vision. This means that leaders need more than just a dream for the future. For their constituents to view them as inspiring, leaders must be able to communicate their visions in ways that encourage constituents to sign up for the duration. Enthusiasm and excitement are essential and signal that a leader is personally committed to pursuing the goal. You cannot be plastic here. You must be genuine and demonstrate knowledge and commitment beyond just a few words. For example, you can't just tell constituents, "I feel great," and expect them to see you as inspiring. Instead, constituents will see you as inspiring when you demonstrate:

- *Passion:* Think about someone who recently motivated you to try something new. Was that person superficial? Did they motivate you by just stating the facts or woodenly describing the process? In most cases, the answer to both questions is "no." Instead, their passion is most likely what made you decide to try it. Deep passion is contagious and passionate leaders are likely to be viewed by their constituents as inspiring. Superficiality will not inspire others.

- *Enthusiasm:* Passion is a deep feeling, but it can sometimes be negative. Many people can passionately discuss why they do not like a certain politician or sports team. In most cases, you hear them with indulgence and walk away. However, when someone's passion is discussed with a positive enthusiasm, you are not as likely to walk away. Instead, you are likely to be caught up with what they're saying. So, too, will your constituents be caught up in your vision when you are both enthusiastic and passionate.

- *Energy:* How often are you inspired by someone who is listless or appears to be tired? My guess is not often. For constituents to believe that you are inspiring, you must radiate energy. This shows them you are motivated and actively seeking the successful attainment of your vision.

- *Positive attitude:* As with enthusiasm, a positive message is what gets people going. If you energetically demonstrate your passion and enthusiasm in a positive way, your constituents will be inspired to follow you and contribute to your vision.

- *Ability to be a cheerleader:* Kouzes and Posner have found that, "We expect our leaders to be enthusiastic, energetic, and positive about the future…a bit of a cheerleader."[23] It is not enough to simply communicate your vision with passion, enthusiasm, and energy. You must also have the ability to encourage those who are following you. It is not always easy to stand on the sidelines and cheer on your team when you might want to be out on the field, but this is essential in order to truly inspire others.

- *Confidence:* Think of the adage, "Never let them see you sweat." Of course, your constituents must see you sweat as you work hard, but that sweat must be associated with activity and not from fear or lack of confidence. Followers like their leaders to be confident—to show assurance of success and strength.

Demonstrating that you can inspire others might seem intimidating at first, but it really isn't that difficult when you truly commit to your organization's missions and goals. Think of the Statue of Liberty and the blue sky above her and focus. Think of your dream and your next steps. Face your weaknesses and figure out a way to eliminate them or, if they are not easily done away with, turn them into strengths. When you do this and show passion, enthusiasm, energy, a positive attitude, and confidence, your constituents will view you as inspiring. Combine that with being honest, competent and forward-looking, and your constituents will see you as credible.

---

[23] Kouzes and Posner, 2003.

## Honest, Competent, Forward-Looking, and Inspiring: Jamie Dimon

In an August 29, 2004 interview with the *New York Times*, Andrea Redmond, co-leader of the C.E.O. and board services practice at executive recruitment firm Russell Reynolds Associates and co-author of the book, *Business Evolves, Leadership Endures* (Easton Studio Press), stated she believed that Jamie Dimon, formerly of Bank One, was a leader who could establish trust with his followers.[*]

According to an article in *Fortune*, Dimon's management style combines ultraconservative principles and a hyperactive, intrusive, frequently improvisational drive to know everything he can. He relentlessly collects information by talking to as many people as possible at every level of the organization. At headquarters, he spends half the day walking the halls, quizzing his executives and grilling office managers, systems analysts, sales representatives and even customers. For Dimon, it's the best way to uncover hidden problems and learn the detailed mechanics of how every business runs.

Dimon's vigilance has advantages. When he was at Travelers Group, "He understood the minutiae of every business, from how clearing works to underwriting asset-backed

*Continues on next page*

### Credibility: It's Key

If we don't believe in the messenger, we won't believe in the message. Therefore, credibility is critical to inspirational leadership. Being credible means being believable and being able to obtain loyalty, commitment, energy, and productivity. Kouzes and Posner go so far as to say that credibility is the cornerstone of leadership. This is because when leaders have high credibility, constituents:

- Are proud to be part of the organization
- Exhibit strong team spirit
- Have values that are consistent with the organization
- Are attached and committed
- Feel a sense of ownership

You might think that credibility can be easily accomplished. After all, doesn't everyone want to be credible? However, the reality is that it is hard to achieve today because people have different criteria for credibility. It must be earned minute by minute, hour by hour and can be lost easily. Credibility is not something that you can apply to specific situations. It is a lifestyle.

Truly credible leaders must continually strive to reflect that they are believable and that they can achieve loyalty, commitment, energy, and productivity by eliminating the barriers between their constituents and themselves. You can do this by:

- Allowing and encouraging your constituents to provide you with feedback (even negative feedback) and make this action the norm.
- Establishing an environment within your organization that encourages and promotes teaching.
- Demonstrating that you care about your constituents by asking appropriate questions and responding to their needs.
- Being visible and available.

The relationships of trust and mutual respect that you create when you eliminate barriers between you and you constituents are paramount in ensuring a bold organization. Leaders who lead with "credibility" promote not just their own success, but cultivate the traits in their followers that will help them succeed as well. They are indeed inspirational leaders.

## What's Next

If you are feeling daunted by the expectations that constituents will have of you as a leader, you can stop right now. The good news is that you don't have to be born an inspirational leader. Perhaps some inspirational leaders inherently know how followers will feel about them and act with instinctive credibility. But many others have learned how to be inspirational leaders. The next chapter looks at how leaders learn to be credible inspirational leaders.

## On the Elevator

A bold organization requires leadership. Leaders must challenge the process, inspire a shared vision, enable others to act, model the way, and encourage the heart. However, it is also important to understand that leadership is a reciprocal process between those who choose to lead and those who choose to follow.

You cannot have leadership without constituents. Therefore, to understand leadership, you must understand the relationship between leaders and constituents. In the 1980s and 1990s, James Kouzes and Barry Posner conducted a study that asked people to take 20 leadership characteristics and rank their top four. The results were: honest, competent, forward-looking and inspiring.

*Honest:* Constituents measure honesty not by what we say, but by what we do. They are seeking consistency between word and deed. They want leaders to practice what they preach. The words they relate to honesty are trust, truthful, standards, principled, values, and ethics.

*Competent:* Leaders must be capable and effective. Constituents want to follow someone with a record of achievements. Leadership competence does not necessarily refer to abilities in the core technology of the opera-

securities," marvels commercial business chief Jim Boshart. "It's the same at Bank One." No amount of fuzzy, feel-good talk, however polished, will fool Dimon. If the facts are bad, he usually knows already. At the same time, Dimon inspires fierce loyalty in his constituents. He forges personal bonds with hundreds of people in every company he runs. "Everyone at Travelers felt they had a personal relationship with him," says Steve Black, a Travelers alumnus who's now chief of equities at J.P. Morgan Chase. Most of all, troops follow Dimon because he's an inspiring leader who prizes results, not politics. "He'll drive you crazy, but I'd trust him with my life," says Miller, whom Dimon hired at Primerica in 1991.[l]

[k] "Buffing the Image of the Chief Executive," *New York Times*, 29 Aug. 2004, http://www.russreyn.com/2005/leadership/rrb_news_2004_0829.html

[l] Shawn Tully, "The Dealmaker and the Dynamo," *Fortune*, February 2004, http://www.mutualofamerica.com/articles/Fortune/February04/fortune2.asp

tion. The words that constituents relate to competency are: capable, effective, asking good questions, achievements, winning track record, leadership skills.

*Forward-looking:* A vision, a dream, a calling, a goal—whatever it is, it is clear that before constituents sign up they want to know where they are heading. They want their leaders to be the "magnetic north" that provides others with the capacity to chart their course toward the future. The words related to forward looking are: vision, dream, goal, planning, strategic, and charting the course.

*Inspiring:* It is not enough to have a dream about the future; you must be able to inspire constituents to sign up. Leaders need to be able to communicate their visions in ways that encourage constituents to sign up for the duration. The words that constituents relate to inspiring are: passion, enthusiastic, energetic, positive, cheerleader, and confidence.

The law of leadership is: If we don't believe in the messenger, we won't believe in the message. When you are honest, competent, forward-looking and inspiring, you are also credible. Being credible means being believable and being able to obtain loyalty, commitment, energy, and productivity. When leaders have high credibility, constituents:

- Are proud to be part of the organization.
- Have a strong team spirit.
- Have values consistent with an organization.
- Feel attached and committed.
- Have a sense of ownership.

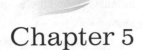

# Chapter 5

# THE LIFE OF AN INSPIRATIONAL LEADER

"A revolution is more than simply reorganizing existing fortresses. Instead, revolutions are grassroots efforts that come from within that transform the culture where the fortresses reside."

By now you're probably wondering just how you can become an inspirational leader. The answer begins with what you think of yourself. You must believe that you are a leader. This belief is the foundation for becoming an inspirational leader. The next step is to understand what inspirational leaders do, because once you know, you can model your behavior accordingly and be well on your way to becoming one.

Succeeding as an inspirational leader involves a combination of learning, teaching, revolutionary practices, and motivation. This chapter addresses what leaders do and shows you how to grow into an inspirational leader.

## What Do Leaders Do?

Over the years, many authors have argued this question and have not come to any real agreement. I have read their books, made my own observations, educated myself, and experienced the benefits of working with inspirational leaders at Tompkins Associates and at client companies. Here's my answer: Leaders prepare their organizations for change—they teach, they create revolutions, and they constantly challenge the status quo to make things happen. When they see an opportunity, they make it happen. They create revolutions by abandoning the past, seeing reality, setting up the present, building for the future, and inspiring the appropriate responses to change with new approaches, methods and products. They also realize that certainty and complacency are two of the biggest enemies of creativity and positive change.

Leaders do not dictate specific behavior, issue orders, or demand compliance. Instead, they get others to see a situation as it really is and to understand what responses need to be taken so that they will act in ways that will move the organization forward.

In the short-term, leaders prepare organizations to change because, with the world changing so quickly, organizations must respond just as quickly. For the long-term, leaders create organizations that can sustain success—a type of success that is achieved by developing other leaders. To do this, leaders draw on a combination of:

- **Vision:** Great leaders can envision with clarity what their organizations must do to win in the global marketplace. They focus on customer needs, technology, competitors, and other external factors. They monitor their competencies, past failures and successes, and their current environment. They consistently update visions to meet the challenges and opportunities that come with change, setting a direction for everyone while considering strategy, structure, and implementation. To do this they touch emotions and drive their vision home with words and actions.

- **Values:** Great organizations and weak organizations alike are happy to tell you that they have values. Often, these values are the same. For example, what organization doesn't value honesty or teamwork? The difference is that the weak organizations pay lip service to values (such as writing a mission statement or putting up posters) so that they can look good to potential customers or clients, but they do not practice them. Once they're on the wall, it is business as usual. Great organizations, however, are deeply concerned about their values. Their leaders pursue a rigorous course of applying these values to their business using the following practices:

  - Clearly articulating their values up front.
  - Continually reviewing their values to make sure they match goals.
  - Using their own behavior to demonstrate their values.
  - Encouraging others to apply their values to their behavior and decisions.
  - Robustly confronting and handling ignorance and resistance.
  - Using their values to develop more leaders.

- **Energy:** Great leaders are very energetic. They throw themselves into whatever they do. They are determined to do good things. They see everything as an opportunity to change and grow. This energy comes from within. It is contagious and everyone around them seems to draw on the strength of their enthusiasm, excitement, and commitment and become energetic themselves.

  Great leaders also turn negative energy to positive uses. They use negatives as teaching opportunities and treat mistakes as learning experiences. They also see negative energy as a way to establish improvements and changes that can generate even more energy. To energize, great leaders use:

  - *A sense of urgency*—Urgency that people can see and feel. They think of competitive threats and opportunities and draw the dire consequences of inaction in a verbal picture that others will immediately understand.

- *A spirit of teamwork*—The communication that everyone is in this together.
- *Confidence in others*—The realistic expectation that the team can reach the goals set.

- **Edge:** Great leaders never take the easy way out. They are willing to leave the security of today, face facts and make tough calls. Risk and pain do not deter them. They show courage based on their convictions. This allows them to tell the truth and admit to their mistakes publicly—the ultimate test of facing reality. Jack Welch, the former CEO of General Electric called this attribute "edge."[24] Edge is about pursuing new business and getting out of old business, promoting risk-taking, and confronting failure.

- **People edge:** There is another edge that great leaders have called the people edge. This is an edge with a personal twist, because it sometimes involves giving people tough feedback about how they're doing and what they value. Noel Tichey, the author of *The Leadership Engine*, describes how Jack Welch used a simple matrix to determine how to use the people edge.[25] I have recreated my own version in Figure 1.

|  | Delivers on commitments | Does not deliver |
|---|---|---|
| Shares values | I | III |
| Does not share values | IV | II |

FIGURE 1. PEOPLE EDGE MATRIX.

In the matrix, Roman numeral I represents a person who shares company values and delivers on commitments. II is someone who does neither. These people are easy to deal with—the first is thanked for his performance and usually moves up in the organization. II is asked to leave. The other two require people edge—III shares company values but does not deliver on commitments and IV delivers on commitments but does not share company values. III should be given a second chance with honest feedback about performance and failure to deliver. IV requires people edge. In other words, IV should be thanked for performance but told to go. This should be done honestly but without cruelty. This is what is meant by people edge.

---

[24] Noel M. Tichey, *The Leadership Engine: How Winning Companies Build Leaders at Every Level.* (New York: Harper Business, 1997), pp. 21.

[25] Tichey, *Leadership Engine*, pp. 164.

## Energizing the Organization

Energy is critical to inspirational leadership and it comes from your passion for people and your personal energy. I've put together a series of questions to help you with this task. The first set of questions is related to assessing your energy. You should ask yourself:

- What energizes me the most?
- What de-energizes me the most?
- How can I raise my personal energy?
- How can I enhance energy boosters and remove energy blockers?

The second set of questions is related to energizing others. A key to energizing people is to set a tone of immediacy to handle change. Define a specific change that you would like to create. Then, answer these questions.

- GOAL: What goal will I set? How will I make the goal worthy of striving for? How will I connect the goal to people on a level that is important to them as individuals without being vague?
- TEAMWORK: How will I instill a sense that we are all (including myself) preparing for change?
- CONFIDENCE: How will I give people the confidence that can help them overcome their fears?

Focusing on the answers to these questions will energize people and your organization.

Leaders use this combination of vision, values, energy, edge, people edge and stories to not only accomplish their goals but also inspire others to challenge the status quo and turn challenges into opportunities. They also recognize that they must never stop learning or teaching and that they must create and lead revolutions, all the while motivating others.

### Leaders are Learners

Leadership is an art—a performing art—and the instrument in the performance is self. Mastery of leadership comes when you master yourself, just as a quest for leadership is a quest for yourself. Therefore, leadership development is a process of self-development from which springs the confidence to lead. This is because you cannot elevate others until you have first elevated yourself through learning.

Leaders are, first and foremost, learners. They draw from their pasts and reflect on their experiences to develop lessons for the future. Inspirational leaders are always looking for ways to improve themselves by reading and studying. Although they see all opportunities as avenues to learning, they also recognize that there are three major opportunities for learning. These opportunities are, in order of importance:

1. Trial and error
2. Observation of others
3. Education

### Trial and Error

In Chapter 2, I mentioned that inspirational leadership is an acquired skill that can't be learned by sitting on the sidelines. You can only learn it by doing—by trying new ideas and gaining knowledge from those ideas that pan out and those that fail. You should also engage with others to get things done and approach situations as if you were a constituent as well as a leader. As you find things that work, add them to your secrets of success. This is what learning to lead by trial and error means.

Learning by trial and error also means that you must stretch and always remain challenged. Arm yourself with a diversity of responsibility and experience. Developing leadership opportunities outside of the workplace, such as in church, sports, the community, and so on, are excellent opportunities to grow. At the same time, examine everything you do. Unexamined responsibilities and experiences don't produce the rich insights that come with reflection and analysis. Instead, you should reflect on what has happened and what you might do differently.

*Observation of Others*

While it is important to examine yourself and your actions to become a leader, it is also important to observe others. Consider people you know, as well as historical or current figures you don't know. Who do you see as inspirational? Who would you follow? What managers in your company and elsewhere are inspirational leaders? Who among your peers do you see as a leader? Who are your role models? Why? This last question is imperative—there have to be reasons, usually based on their actions, for why you believe these people are inspirational. Use these reasons as part of your quest to learn.

It's also important for you to consider people whom you believe are not good leaders. After all, we can all learn from the bad as well as the good. Think of leadership styles that turn you off. Why? Once you have identified these behaviors, make a mental note not to follow them.

*Education*

Although there are great lessons in leadership to be learned on the job, there are just as many to be learned in a more formal educational setting such as a classroom or online course. Inspirational leaders believe that their formal education is never complete. There is always something else that you can learn from a teacher, a book, a group or a university. Inspirational leaders continually educate themselves, seeking areas for improvement through books and courses that can help them better themselves as leaders and people.

The first step to finding education is to determine your needs. Do not wait for others to tell you. Assess your thoughts and weaknesses and how they affect your leadership abilities. Use self-reflection and really listen to your inner voice. You should also make a list of practices you'd like to know more about—create an inventory. And although you shouldn't wait for others to tell you what you need to work on, do ask for feedback. You might have missed something.

Once you have your inventory, initiate your learning agenda. You can pursue your education through a combination of classes, reading and self-study. Additional options include taking courses on tape or online and finding books and other tools that address your needs. As you learn, you will realize that this knowledge needs to be shared with others, because

# Leadership Lessons

You are the best person to determine what you need to learn. However, there are a few basic lessons that apply to all leaders:

- Leaders don't wait. They focus on quick wins, immediate action, and gaining momentum.
- Character counts: True leaders are honest, forward-looking, inspiring, and competent. They have credibility and values, and you can believe what they say.
- Leaders have their heads in the clouds and their feet on the ground. In other words, they not only have a vision for the future, but they have a sense of direction that will get them to that vision.
- Shared values make a difference. True leaders present values that are consistent with those of their constituents.
- Leaders can't do it alone. Personal best means *our* personal best, not my personal best.
- The legacy that leaders leave behind is the life they lead. You lead by deeds that make you a role model and set the pace. The best way to do this is to do what you say you will do.
- Leadership is everyone's business. Everyone is a leader in some circumstance.

one of the most basic premises of inspirational leadership is not only being able to lead, but also enabling others to lead.

## Leaders are Teachers

True leadership not only fulfills desired goals today, it also focuses on sustainability. Leaders are continually redefining goals to changing circumstances and they cannot do this without other leaders. Therefore, great leaders surround themselves with other leaders and they also work to develop others in this role. There are a number of approaches you can use to develop leaders. I have taken the most common approaches—command, tell, sell, and teach—and organized them based on their effectiveness (Figure 2) as related to depth of learning, level of commitment, amount of time required, and the capacity to grow more leaders.

In the command approach, leaders issue directives and mandates—there is no teachable point of view. This method takes the least amount of time, but is not likely to develop more leaders. The depth of learning is low and there is no growth in human capital. There is little commitment and understanding because being ordered to do something does not inspire buy-in.

The tell approach is a little more successful. In this approach, leaders use instruction—much like they are teachers in a school. They deliver their teachable point of view and expect their students to adopt it. All actions will be based on this common point of view. The time required for this approach is a little higher than for command. The problem is that the leader is still telling followers what to do without including them in the process as anything other than students. This does not inspire commitment and understanding and there is little depth of learning. While you might have a slightly higher capacity to grow leaders than the command method, it is still very low. You are not likely to develop other inspirational leaders with this approach.

The sell approach involves more than instruction. Leaders persuade their followers that their point of view is correct. They might involve the followers to a small extent,

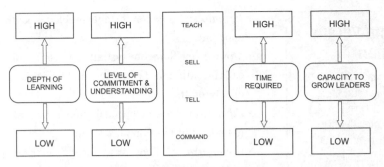

FIGURE 2. APPROACHES TO TEACHING.

erhaps with a limited amount of participation or presenting a small number of options. hey are salesmen who are using pseudo-involvement to force others to buy in to their roduct, which, in this case, is their teaching point of view. Leaders who use the sell ap- roach create customers—people who have "bought" a point of view. The result is that epth of understanding (it's not difficult to understand a sales pitch) and commitment night be higher than with the tell approach, but the capacity to grow leaders is not high nough and a lot of time is spent to produce customers rather than leaders.

The teach approach results in the highest depth of understanding, commitment and apacity to grow leaders. Rather than instructing, telling or persuading others to follow neir teachable point of view, they encourage others to develop their own. This creates a pirit of cooperative learning that breeds confident action and starts a cycle of teaching nat leads to more leaders. The teach approach is not easy, and it is a long-term process. 'ou must be prepared to commit a lot of time and energy. The rewards are immeasur- ble, however, because your organization will be filled with inspirational leaders who vill engage others and lead a revolution that results in long-term organizational success.

The teach approach is best from an inspirational leadership perspective, but it is not lways appropriate. For example, there are times when immediate action is required— quipment or hardware failure, not receiving a shipment of critical parts in time, or a iatural disaster to name a few—where, instead of teaching a point of view, you need to ise the command approach because of the lack of time caused by the situation at hand. n other situations, tell or sell might work better. Therefore, it is critical to understand vhich approach is appropriate for your particular situation—being bold means applying he right approach at the right time.

## eaders and Revolutions

True organizational success requires a revolution. Organizational revolution is a rocess of preemptively initiating change to meet transformations that occur in the mar- etplace, and it usually follows this pattern:

# Leadership versus Management

To be a good leader, you must understand leaders versus management. For example:

- Leaders seek growth while management seeks control.
- Leaders innovate while management administrates.
- Leaders rely on people and trust while management relies on systems and controls.
- Leaders ask what and why while management asks how and when.™

Leaders might need to both lead and manage, but not one at the expense of the other. The chart below highlights more of the differences between leadership and management.

| Management | Leadership |
|---|---|
| Control | Change— Growth |
| Know where they are | Know where they are going |
| Who are you? | What do you do? |
| Boss of people | Servant of people |
| Accountable for results and people | Hold people accountable for results |
| Focus on bottom line | Focus on horizon |
| People doing it right | People doing the right thing |

*Continues on next page*

- *Irritation:* An uncomfortable problem becomes apparent.
- *Motivation:* Someone, usually an inspirational leader calls attention to the problem and holds out the vision of solving it.
- *Education:* Those who suffer under the problem seek to understand its complex nature.
- *Collaboration:* Those who understand the problem and are still convinced they can solve it bind together to develop a powerful force. They collectively plan a strategy for formulating a solution to the problem.
- *Action:* The motivated, educated group carries out its plan to solve the problem.

A successful revolution has a grassroots element and a leadership element. However, leadership is the key element of a revolution because grassroots energy without proper leadership, or with poor or corrupt leadership, becomes merely a fringe element. Grassroots energy channeled by solid leadership becomes a movement with permanent, lasting results—which means they continue the revolution.

A revolution is more than simply reorganizing existing fortresses. Instead, revolutions are grassroots efforts that come from within that transform the culture where the fortresses reside. Culture is an organization's personality; it is how things work in the organization. Over time, your organization's culture has evolved; however, when you lead a revolution, you are shaping the evolution rather than waiting for it to happen. Your goal is to instill an attitude of dynamic consistency—a mentality of continuous improvement based on a clear, shared and consistent direction of where the organization is headed.

Because of the nature of the cultural transformation, a revolution cannot be managed; it must be led. This includes defining its direction. Without a robust definition of direction, insufficient evidence will exist for true buy-in.

This definition of direction must have:

- A vision
- A mission
- Requirements of success
- Guiding principles
- Evidence of success

The first two elements, vision and mission, are closely linked. The vision addresses where you are headed; it is your goal. The mission addresses how you will get there; it is your strategy. The mission is also your plan for accomplishing your vision.

The requirements of success answer three questions:

1. What is the science of our revolution?
2. What are the rules of our game?
3. What are the paradigms in which we believe?

It is critical that everyone in your revolution understands the requirements of success. This is because they form the science of your revolution. If you and your organization do not understand your revolution and what it needs to be successful, this can spell trouble.

Guiding principles are a set of standards about how people should be treated. These standards are deep seated and pervasive and they influence all that you do—judgments, opinions, attitudes, desires, fears, responses and actions. They play a big role in defining the spirit in which things in your revolution will be accomplished. As individuals contemplate different actions, they consciously and subconsciously compare the alternatives to these standards to define the right path.

The evidence of success describes how you will measure the success of your revolution. Measurements are what provide leaders the information they need to provide feedback on the revolution. They allow you to determine whether you are on the right course, whether you need to re-double your efforts, or whether you should follow a different course.

In *Revolution: Take Charge Strategies for Business Success*, I describe how you can develop a vision, a mission, requirements for success, guiding principles

| Management | Leadership |
|---|---|
| Controlling performance | Defining motivation |
| Administrates | Innovates |
| Relies on system and controls | Relies on people and trust |

* Jim Tompkins, *Revolution: Take Charge Strategies for Business Success.* (Raleigh, NC: Tompkins Press, 1998), pp. 93.

and evidence of success. After you have developed them, create a process for achieving alignment. In other words, for people to sign up for your revolution, they must know what they are signing up for. You cannot just develop the above items and hang them on the wall as a mission statement or model of success poster. Just like the previous discussion on values, without a process for alignment, the model of success is just public relations. Alignment is behavioral and emotional interconnectedness; it is acting as one. To achieve alignment, leaders clearly communicate where their revolutions are taking them. This is part of another critical role of a leader—to *motivate*.

## Leaders Motivate

A recurring theme in our discussion is that true leaders exhibit a high level of energy, intensity, passion and determination. They channel this energy and direct it toward others to motivate them into making a vision a reality and becoming inspirational leaders. They draw on their inner and outer characters to motivate in four ways:
- How they think (inner character)
- How they communicate (outer character)
- How they work (outer character)
- How they treat people (outer character)

*Leaders Motivate by How They Think*

Leadership is not a set of personality traits; however, all genuine leaders have six key qualities that represent the essence of this role. These qualities define the leader's inner character and actions:
- **Integrity:** Integrity means telling and living the truth. Leaders deal with people and situations sincerely and straightforwardly and do not compromise on what they believe to be true. Integrity demands the specification of ethical behavior and the elimination of games-playing and cheating. Integrity also demands that there be honesty in all dealings, where honesty is measured by consistency of word and deed. It is from this honesty that trust and loyalty spring.
- **Credibility:** Credibility is related to integrity but takes the idea a step further. Credibility means being accountable, genuine and open. Credibility must be earned over time in painstaking increments and it can easily be lost. It means being clear, precise, and accurate in all interactions so that there are no misunderstandings or misinterpretations.
- **Enthusiasm:** There is a misconception that leaders and managers should leave their excitement about work and life at home when they are at the office. But this will not motivate anyone. Instead, to motivate, leaders must unleash their excitement and enthusiasm. If you want people to be excited, you must first be excited.

This is because enthusiasm is contagious! Plant inspirational enthusiasm and watch it grow.

- **Optimism:** From enthusiasm comes optimism--an incurable condition of people who focus on success. It comes from an inner confidence. It is this confidence that keeps you from obsessing over minor setbacks and keeps you focused on the path forward.
- **Urgency:** The future can only be addressed by what we do today. Leaders must act with a sense of urgency so that their organization will act with a sense of urgency—the time for action is now. For example, I use a salutation—GO! GO! GO!—to convey my desire for action, my encouragement, and my belief that anything worth doing is worth doing now.
- **Determination:** Leaders demonstrate determination by stepping forward in times of uncertainty. They exhibit the courage to step into the unknown—to try new and different solutions to problems or to steer a company toward a new course. They take charge and have high expectations.

*Leaders Motivate by How They Communicate*

Communication style is one of the things that define outer character. Leaders view communication from the receiver's perspective. Their focus is on the receipt of a message and not the generation of that message. This means that communication is not just what leaders say. It is also what they don't say, how they say what they say, and how they act in general—all of this impacts the receipt of the message. To do this, leaders use empathy and simple communications.

Empathy is characterized by "feeling with another" and not just "feeling for another." It means putting yourself in another person's shoes. Empathy allows leaders to be open and sensitive to others. They realize that all people are unique and that everyone has the potential to receive the same message differently. This is why simple communications are what leaders use to motivate. Simple communications eliminate ambiguity and are characterized by:

- Simple language that stays clear of complex words and phrases.
- Simple mini-memos that present a problem/solution/action path.
- Simple persuasion techniques that state facts and conclusions simply, using logical steps (1-2-3).
- Simple life philosophies that show your true self—always.

*Leaders Motivate by How They Work*

Leaders who wish to improve the quality and quantity of work within their organization model work excellence themselves. There are two rules pertaining to work that leaders practice: (1) Work hard and smart and (2) Enjoy work. Working hard and smart is how you gain credibility and energy in the eyes of your constituents. Working hard and smart means:

- Making the right decision at the right time and communicating it to the right people.
- Reducing emphasis on time-management so that interruptions that are part of the day become a chance to teach and not annoyances or detriments to progress.
- Paying attention to the right details by involving yourself only with the details you need to know for a decision you are making and not getting buried or distracted.
- Going the extra mile by exceeding expectations, really listening, questioning deeply, being friendly, being real, being more responsive than people think possible, and treating every interaction as if your credibility is on the line, as probably is the case.
- Keeping your thinking loose so that you can accept change and mistakes.

Enjoying work is the second part of how leaders motivate by how they work. There are four things a leader does to enjoy work personally:

- Grow as a person: A leader's personal growth is important to how he or she enjoys work and motivates: First, the leader derives personal satisfaction from individual learning and thus enjoys work. Second, the leader's personal growth sets the pace for the rest of the organization's learning. Third, it ignites new ideas and new thinking throughout the organization.
- Be a realist: When leaders are realists, they enjoy work because they are not being beaten down or sidelined by trying to make the impossible possible. Using intellectual honesty, they set realistic goals that can be met, increasing job satisfaction and enjoyment.
- Be natural: There is no fun in being phony. When leaders are themselves, they enjoy work and life because they are not playing a difficult, unfamiliar role. When leaders are accessible, predictable, open, compassionate, and caring, they have personal satisfaction that spills over to how they feel about work.
- Have fun: When you have fun at work, then you are enjoying it. It's that simple. Therefore, leaders show that they enjoy work by being positive, celebrating successes, saying thank you, and laughing. This is contagious and spills over into the organization, motivating others to do their best so that they can continue the fun.

### Leaders Motivate by How They Treat People

How leaders treat people has a big impact on motivating others. A genuine leader treats others the way they want to be treated. This has much to do with compassion, politeness, courtesy, trust, dignity, respect and fairness. This can be done by following ten simple principles:

- Like yourself: You must have a positive self image before you can have a positive image of others.
- Accept others: Accept others as they are and not as you would like them to be. Love diversity, and above all, love people.
- Respect others: Everyone is unique and merits your appreciation, honor, and respect.
- Trust others: Demonstrating your trust in others encourages them to be trustworthy and makes them trust you.
- Think "we": Outstanding performance is the result of a "we mentality" and not the "I" mentality.
- Be real: You are a real person with feelings, concerns, and interests—just like everyone else. Demonstrate your realness by socializing, participating in small talk and conversations, and being yourself.
- Say "Thank You": Truly appreciate people helping you. Say "thank you" as often as you can throughout the day—but do it with sincerity so that those you thank do not feel as if it is automatic lip service.
- Anger slowly, or not at all: If you have a temper, you must try not to show it.
- Encourage others: Know when to give people a pat on the back or a pep talk. Be available when people need you and your support.
- Be a nice person: Be liked because you are gentle, kind and considerate.

## What's Next

The secret to sustaining involvement and passion in a **bold** organization is the commitment and enthusiasm of its leaders. They have a vision, values, energy, edge, people edge, and stories and they learn, teach, create revolutions, and motivate. They are courageous, charting unknown courses and making tough calls for the sake of organizational success. Upcoming chapters examine one of the new courses businesses embark upon today—outsourcing—and the tough calls that bold leaders of bold organizations must make to stay competitive in the marketplace.

## On the Elevator

Being an inspirational leader means believing that you are a leader, understanding what leaders do, and learning, teaching, creating revolutions, and motivating. Inspirational leaders prepare their organizations for change and they constantly challenge the status quo to make things happen. When they see an opportunity, they make it happen by drawing on a combination of:

- Vision: What it takes to win.
- Values: What they live by.

## Don't Forget Yourself

When you are thinking about treating others as they would like to be treated, you should not forget yourself. You also need to treat yourself the way you would like to be treated. Here are some tips for making sure that you treat yourself well:

- Manage stress: Watch for signs of stress such as forgetfulness, fatigue, changes in appetite, and back pain.
- Gain control where you can: Look for areas that you can control and then control them.
- Balance: If you feel like a victim, try to figure out why. Perhaps you are a perfectionist or maybe you use people.
- Take a 15-minute break each day: Reflect on the big picture.
- Do what you love: Love your job or find one that you do love.
- Focus on your strengths: Do what you do well and try to do more of it.
- Have a mentor or coach: Ask the question: "Who are my teachers today?"
- Get out of your comfort zone: Go for risk. Do things differently.
- Have a healthy support system: Have a personal board of directors that you can vent to or share ideas with.
- Learn to say no: Quit doing something.
- Think about the customer: What can you do for your customer today?

*Continues on next page*

- Energy: What they use to inspire others.
- Edge: Making difficult decisions and showing the courage of their convictions.
- People edge: Giving people tough feedback about how they're doing.

Leaders are, first and foremost, learners. Although they see all opportunities as learning opportunities, they also recognize that there are three major opportunities for learning:

1. Trial and error: Learning by doing, engaging with others, and gaining experience.
2. Observation of others: Watching great leaders and the impacts their actions have on others.
3. Education: Classroom. Reading. Self-study.

One of the basic premises of inspirational leadership is not only being able to lead but also teaching others to do so. There are a number of approaches you can use to develop leaders. The most common approaches are command, tell, sell, and teach, but teach is the only approach that will lead to the high depth of understanding, the commitment, and the capacity to grow more leaders that is necessary for a bold organization and the revolution that creates it.

Leadership is the most important element of a revolution because grassroots energy without proper leadership, or with poor or corrupt leadership, becomes merely a fringe element. Grassroots energy channeled by solid leadership becomes a movement with permanent lasting results—which means they continue the revolution. To achieve alignment, leaders clearly communicate where their revolutions are taking them. This is part of another critical role of a leader—to motivate.

Leaders draw on their inner and outer characters to motivate in four ways:

- How they think: All genuine leaders have six key qualities that represent the essence of the leader. They are integrity, credibility, enthusiasm, optimism, urgency, and determination.
- How they communicate: Leaders view communication from the receiver's perspective. Their focus is

on the receipt of a message and not the generation of that message. They use empathy and simple communications.

- How they work: Leaders who wish to improve the quality and quantity of work within their organization will model that work excellence themselves. There are two rules pertaining to work that leaders practice: (1) Work hard and smart and (2) Enjoy work.
- How they treat people: A genuine leader treats others the way they want to be treated—with compassion, politeness, courtesy, trust, dignity, respect, and fairness.

- Be healthy: Are you healthy?
- Define personal purpose: Why do you get up in the morning?
- Focus on the spiritual: Be right with yourself.
- Spend time with good people: Be around spiritual leaders.
- Lighten up: Smile. No day is so bad that you can't find something positive about it or a reason to laugh.

# Part 2

## Outsourcing:
## A Bold Move

# Chapter 6
# DEFINING CORE COMPETENCIES AND OUTSOURCING TARGETS

"There are a number of companies that have become casualties of poor outsourcing campaigns. The good news is that this doesn't have to happen."

As demonstrated in the previous chapter, courage and spirit ("edge") are at the heart of being an inspirational leader. This is because to lead a bold organization, you must be willing to take risks and make tough decisions.

To be bold, your company will have to make significant changes in the way it conducts business so that it grows and thrives in today's accelerated environment. This means looking at the big picture and searching for the parts of that picture that are just filling up canvas and not adding value to the subject. It means defining core competencies, and outsourcing those activities that are not value-add, or that are taking your attention as a leader away from those functions and processes that create profit and give you the edge to keep you ahead in the global marketplace.

## Outsourcing Defined

Outsourcing is a management tool that shifts the organizational structure of companies. It is a business transformation process that can create great opportunity for improved performance. It reduces work and improves the efficiency and effectiveness of processes. Because some of the biggest names in business are outsourcing, it is often viewed as the source of higher profitability and larger market share.

Bold organizations that approach outsourcing with business process knowledge and effective processes can reap its full benefits. The trick is to pursue it with careful planning and complete understanding of business processes and core competencies. This chapter discusses the benefits of outsourcing (why a bold organization should outsource), explains core functions (and how they relate to core competency), and shows you how to define your outsourcing targets.

## Why Outsource?

Outsourcing is a risky enterprise, and if it isn't done correctly, it can hurt a company. There are a number of companies that have become casualties of poor outsourcing campaigns. The good news is that this doesn't have to happen. If you follow the process outlined in this book, your outsourcing venture will be a success, and you will reap the rewards. The benefits of outsourcing can be divided into types. First, there are the direct benefits—those that have an immediate impact. Then, there are the indirect benefits—those that outsourcing has on the processes that have remained in-house.

### Direct Benefits

The direct benefits of outsourcing are those related to reduced costs, reduced cycle times, and customer perception and satisfaction. These benefits are:

- **Focus on core competency:** A company that outsources no longer needs all the resources they have been using to make a product, store it, and get it to the customer. They can redirect these resources to their core functions. For example, if a company has decided that its core competency is product design and engineering only, outsourcing the product's manufacture means that the design and engineering can only get better, because that is now the company's main focus. Workers will not be spread too thin, managers have time to focus more on the design process, and leaders can concentrate on new engineering and design as opposed to manufacturing and distribution.
- **Reduction in costs:** When a company outsources, it can consolidate operations. The manufacturing company that has decided to focus on product design and engineering and outsource the rest, for instance, no longer has to maintain factories, distribution centers, or inventory. The service provider or providers take care of these elements. Therefore, the manufacturing and distribution costs to the company that has outsourced are lower because they are no longer responsible for physical plants and personnel related to these operations functions. Also, the vendor might be providing a shared service, so the company is not paying for under-utilized capacity, which will lower inventory-carrying costs.
- **Reduction in head count of hourly workers and management:** The kind of streamlined, lean company that succeeds in today's marketplace must do so with fewer employees than the companies of the last generation. Outsourcing is one of the most effective methods for reducing head count. Instead of a mandate that each department must cut 2.5 employees while keeping workload constant or, in many cases, increasing it, entire departments are cut, with the workload going with them. Those departments that will maintain and grow a company's core competencies do not lose valuable personnel or increase responsibilities. In return, the

personnel used by outsourcers are trained workers or professionals, many of whom are stars in their respective functions.

- **Improved accuracy:** Outsourcing narrows the amount of tasks that your company and its employees must accomplish, creating greater focus and less room for errors. When someone (either inside a company or outside it) has only to perform one task, it is likely that if that task involves a count or pay outs, then the result of the completed task will be more accurate. If all you have to do is inventory, then your inventory count is more likely to be accurate than if you have to supervise several plants, pay department bills, maintain a global network of distribution centers, and so on.

- **Flexibility and wider range of service:** If you think that focusing on a core competency and outsourcing the rest might be limiting your company, you might want to think again. If you outsource non-core functions, your company has no limits. You can offer your customers more, because although the company might actually be doing less within its four physical walls, it is accomplishing more. Your company can produce more, ship more, and break into product lines heretofore not considered because there was already too much to do when everything had to be done in-house.

- **Access to global networks and superior technology:** Many outsourcing service providers have been doing what they do best for one or two decades, and some even longer. As they have acquired more clients and become better established, they've built sophisticated relationships and partnerships, and most belong to multilevel networks. When your company hires one of these providers, you have the opportunity of accessing their multilevel logistics networks and using their technology.

- **Improved service:** Outsourcing improves service by shortening cycle times and speeding time to market. This is because tapping into capabilities not available internally increases scheduling flexibility and resource availability, and that reduces the amount of time between production and the customer's doorstep. This ensures higher levels of customer satisfaction.

- **Improved quality:** Many companies that are outsourcing today originally did so to cut costs. However, they have now found that not only can outsourcing reduce overhead, but it can also improve quality. This is because outsourcing providers that run volume operations have better quality assurance (QA) programs in place than the average company that is still trying to do it in-house. The results are less damage, less rework, improved response time to inquiries, and greater inventory accuracy.

- **Reduction in capital investment and cash inflow:** Outsourcing can reduce capital investment. This is because, after functions are outsourced, the facilities previously used by your company for those functions are removed from the balance

## Outsourcing Survey: U.S. Companies Benefit from Outsourcing Experiences

A new survey of top U.S. financial executives by CFO Research shows that American companies are not only pleased with the benefits delivered by current outsourcing efforts, but they also plan to do more outsourcing in the future. Most of the 288 respondents said their own outsourcing initiatives met or exceeded expectations by:

- Enabling their companies to refocus attention on matters that are core to the business (58 percent)
- Improving process speeds (56 percent)
- Providing near-term cost savings (56 percent)

The same study also shows that executives who have outsourced primarily to the U.S. increasingly want options that meet their business objectives. Almost 73 percent of U.S.-based companies plan to outsource more functions in the coming years, and close to 23 percent are interested in outsourcing a broad range of functions and processes. In other words, they are considering outsourcing everything that's not core to their businesses.

Based on the responses to the survey, it seems that U.S.

*Continues on next page*

sheet, and your company can sell them. This makes capital funds more available for your core functions. Outsourcing can also eliminate the need to demonstrate return on equity from capital investments in non-core areas. This can improve certain financial measurements.

*Indirect Benefits*

A company that decides to outsource operations functions often finds that its internal processes benefit from the decision. These are benefits that might not be as obvious as the direct benefits, because they indirectly affect a company's bottom line. Indirect benefits include:

- **Creating a catalyst for change:** In the search for core competencies, how outsourced operations are managed is highlighted. Companies can take a closer look at engineered operations, planning and scheduling. The result is a better grasp of accountability and root cause analysis, which can only improve core functions.

- **Initiating or fueling change:** When a company outsources, it is often able to offer new services and capabilities, because outsourcing has increased performance in the form of shorter lead times and reduction in the landed cost to the customer.

- **Stimulating analysis:** The requirement to document business processes (and their costs) inherent with any outsourcing implementation often uncovers valuable information that can be studied and put to use in your company. In other words, developing metrics to use to select a third-party provider might result in your asking why these metrics aren't used in your company.

- **Converting sluggish functional areas into dynamic, successful ones:** The actual process of finding a provider and performing a baseline analysis will cause a company to look internally to improve processes. This often breathes new life into functions like customer service, purchasing and procurement.

- **Resource and contact development:** After a successful outsourcing implementation, companies often find they have access to new business resources and personnel, such as freight handlers, value-added service providers and IT. Using these contacts, they can form new, beneficial relationships.

When the direct and indirect benefits of outsourcing are laid out, it's easy to see why so many companies have either outsourced already or are planning to do so. Yes, there are risks and yes, there is a possibility that an outsourcing strategy can fail. But if you know how to approach outsourcing or work with someone who has made outsourcing a core competency, the benefits of being a bold organization that outsources far outweigh the risks. The key to the outsourcing opportunity is in your outsourcing strategy—determining your non-core and core functions, identifying your core competencies, defining targets, and managing your outsourcing relationships.

## Non-core versus Core Functions

Business processes can be divided into two types: core functions and non-core functions. Core functions are what a business is all about. Non-core functions are processes that either add significant value to the core product or service, or provide the means for supporting the company and retaining employees (for example, HVAC, security, cleaning, landscaping, payroll, maintenance and so on). Each of these types can be further divided into what type of focus they have: primary or secondary. In other words, there are primary and secondary core functions and primary and secondary non-core functions. This can be illustrated in a simple matrix (Figure 1).

executives now understand that the benefits of outsourcing are more than just reduced costs and spending. They see that outsourcing is a shortcut to business success as companies use it to fuel growth and innovation. In these competitive times, today's executives are looking for ways to drive benefits beyond cost issues to improve corporate performance and shareholder value, and they realize outsourcing is an efficient way to increase competitiveness, improve speed to market and transform their businesses.

Executives also said their companies achieved the best results from outsourcing when they actively managed the process from the beginning with the careful selection of the best partner for the assignment. Respondents said they recognize their success with outsourcing depends on their own governance of the process."

---

" "U.S. Companies Benefit from Outsourcing Experiences, Plan to Expand Efforts, Capgemini Study Shows; As Companies Accelerate Outsourcing Plans, Executives Demand More Options," *Businesswire*, 23 May 2006, http://home.businesswire.com/portal/site/google/index.jsp?ndmViewId=news_view&newsId=20060523005590&newsLang=en

|  | **Primary Focus** | **Secondary Focus** |
|---|---|---|
| **Core Process** | Things that differentiate your organization in the marketplace. The reasons customers come to you. | Things that need to be done well but are not visible to the customer. |
| **Non-Core Process** | Things that if not done well can have a negative impact on your customer relationship. | Things that need to be done but do not have any significant impact on the success of the business. |

FIGURE 1. CORE COMPETENCY MATRIX.

Primary core functions are those that differentiate your company from all the rest; they are the reasons your customers come to you. Consider a "chic" retailer like the Gap. What differentiates them from other companies and brings customers to them? The answers to those questions would most likely be their retail stores, merchandising and brand, as well as their relationship (or touch points) with the customer. You can arrive at similar answers for your company by asking, "If I outsource this function, how will it affect my relationship with the customer?"

Secondary core functions are those activities and processes that must be done well for your company to retain market share, but are not visible to customers. For the retailer just mentioned, the secondary focus core functions are likely to be procurement, sourcing and real estate.

It can be difficult, at times, to distinguish secondary core functions from primary core or even primary non-core. How you touch your customers can help you make the distinction. Customer service is a good example. Some companies outsource it, and some don't. Those who don't outsource customer service have probably decided that customer service is intricately interwoven within their customer's perception of the company—this is the case with a lot of catalog companies and direct marketers. It is one of those functions that you really need to spend some time thinking about. And the more time you spend wondering, the more likely it is to be considered a secondary core, since you could still outsource it.

Primary non-core processes add significant value to your product or service and have an impact on a company's bottom line; they too are noticed by customers. If they are not done well, your bottom line is likely to suffer, although they might not put you out of business altogether. For the retailer, the primary non-core functions could be IT, HR, and logistics.

Secondary non-core functions are those that do not really negatively affect your revenues. They are distinguished from primary and secondary core functions and primary non-core functions by one important difference: they are not driven by your customers. These include payroll, landscaping, food service, security and maintenance. These functions need to be done, but unless they are done really, really poorly, they do not have an impact on an organization's bottom line.

Now, if the food service people poison your staff, the landscape people knock trees onto your facility, the payroll people embezzle your funds, the audit people allow others to misreport your income, or the janitorial people throw away important papers, then, yes, these things will have an impact on your bottom line. But for these functions to do damage to any serious extent, they have to be done really poorly. How many companies do you know that have had trees knocked into their facilities by a landscaping service provider?

To further understand the differences between primary and secondary non-core functions, think of a manufacturing company that has hired outside providers for both landscaping and logistics. If landscaping does not work out, the research organization fires the firm and brings in another provider. If logistics does not work out, the organization has a major sunk cost in the transition costs. Moreover, it has exposed its customers to bad customer service, and it might incur serious interruptions in service. The secondary non-core landscaping mistake is certainly not good, but it will not really have an impact on business. To the contrary, the primary non-core logistics mistakes will have adversely affected the organization's bottom line, and it might well take years to recover from the impacts.

To help make the distinctions in your company's core competencies, take this matrix and apply it. For the retailer, the matrix might look like that shown in Figure 2.

|  | **Primary Focus** | **Secondary Focus** |
|---|---|---|
| **Core Process** | • Retail Stores<br>• Merchandising<br>• Brand | • Procurement<br>• Sourcing<br>• Real Estate |
| **Non-Core Process** | • IT<br>• HR<br>• Logistics | • Store Supplies<br>• Accounting<br>• Landscaping |

FIGURE 2. CORE COMPETENCY MATRIX FOR THE CHIC RETAILER.

When the core and non-core competencies are presented in this way, it makes it simpler to think about what to keep in-house and what to consider outsourcing. Figure 3 shows the matrix again, this time applied to a manufacturing/distribution company:

| | Primary Focus | Secondary Focus |
|---|---|---|
| **Core Process** | • Production<br>• Product Design<br>• Production Planning and Scheduling | • Procurement<br>• Logistics<br>• HR<br>• Maintenance |
| **Non-Core Process** | • IT<br>• Finance and Accounting<br>• Sales and Marketing | • Real Estate<br>• Food Service<br>• Landscaping |

FIGURE 3. CORE COMPETENCY MATRIX FOR A MANUFACTURER/DISTRIBUTOR.

As you can see, the company's core processes are production, product design, production planning, and scheduling, procurement, logistics, HR and maintenance. The company probably could keep all of these functions in-house, but it might not be as profitable as it would if it decided to outsource maintenance and HR. Also, the company could decide that since sales and marketing are non-core that they could outsource that function; however, that might negatively impact the customer's perception of the company.

Why is defining primary and secondary core and non-core competencies so important? The answer to that question is simple: Once these distinctions are made, company leaders can spend their time focusing on what is important to the company's customers and what will most add to the company's success. Currently, corporate leaders do not have enough hours in the day to do all that needs to be done. And, when they sit down and look at what they're spending their time on, they see that much of that time is spent dealing with issues that do not necessarily drive the company's success.

For example, think about how much time is spent gathering and analyzing data before a company sees the result and can take action. Suppose a company looked at its processes and determined that data analysis is not what it does best. So, they found someone else to mine data, analyze it, and provide company leaders with a report full of all the information they need to make informed decisions about their business. The result is that these leaders had much more time to focus on what truly drives their business. Consider NASA. It was founded to run space programs; however, over the years it added such functions as telemetry and tracking facilities to its business activities. These activities consumed a great deal of NASA's time and yet were not really NASA's bailiwick. Imagine the effect on your tax dollars. Now, they outsource these activities and have returned to their core business activity—the thing they do best, which is running U.S. space programs.

It is critical to define core competencies and then to subdivide them into primary and secondary core, constantly asking how each function touches your company. Once that is accomplished, you will have a better picture of what functions you should outsource. But just how do you set about organizing this? Through teamwork, by dividing your company into its different business processes and asking questions about each process.

# Chapter 6: DEFINING CORE COMPETENCIES AND OUTSOURCING TARGETS

## Identifying Core Functions

The first thing to be done in the process of defining core and non-core is to create a team that includes you and at least one inspirational leader from each of the areas defined as main operating functions. This team would probably need about seven to ten people, representing a cross-section across the entire organization. After spending time creating a core competency matrix like those illustrated previously, you and your team can then present the results and a reevaluation process begins. For example, if there is a function that takes up company time that team members believe should have even more time devoted to it, that process may be identified as a primary core function that should not be outsourced. The converse might be true in other situations—if the company is spending a lot of time on logistics that it wants to spend on product innovation, then logistics could be considered a primary non-core function that can be outsourced.

Next, break your company up into discrete processes. One way to do this is to consider your company's relationship with your customers and how they view your company, your products, the effort and materials that go into making it, and then break down the services that support making it. Such a division might include production, IT, administration, logistics, security and marketing/advertising. Another way is to list your company's capabilities, and then assign them to appropriate business processes. The purpose of this task is to make the identification of core competency less daunting. It helps to break a company into manageable chunks and allows a robust focus on all aspects of the business. This also promotes awareness of exactly what goes on in the company and which parts may actually be successful if done outside the company.

In many ways, this task is a brainstorming session. You do not have to get this exactly right at first. As you go through the motions of critically evaluating business processes and support services, you will further define these processes. They can be either consolidated or subdivided depending on availability of service providers on the outside.

A simple example of this is a company that lists distribution and transportation as separate business processes. Later, this company realizes that there is so much overlap between the two that the process might actually be logistics. Or, a company might list production as one of its business processes and then realize that production can be further divided into innovation, design, and manufacturing. Once this task is complete, the discussion of which business process is core and which is not can begin.

After you and your team have divided your company into business processes, there is a set of questions you can ask each other to determine core processes. At this point, you and your team do not have to decide what is primary core and what is secondary core. Instead, try determining your organization's overall core competencies. This set of questions is:

## Determining Your Market Differentiator: Questions to Consider

Charles Brunner, the Director of Product Genesis, a spin off of the MIT Innovation Center, has compiled the following list of questions to ask that can help you define what differentiates your company's products or services from those of your competitors:

- Do you possess or hold an industry position that can be defended and enforced? Will this position limit a competitive threat?
- Do you hold trade secrets that are unique enough to prevent reverse engineering of your products or that are not readily obvious to someone skilled in that area?
- Do you have unique skills that are not easily acquired by your competition?
- What else about your company, products, or services prevents your competitors from eroding your market share?
- What differentiating factor about your company allows you to face threats from the competition in your segment?

Understanding your differentiated competitive position, the makeup of your competency and what defines opportunities for your company

*Continues on next page*

- Who are our customers?
- How do the functions we have defined touch the customer? Or do they touch the customer at all?
- What is it that our customers know us for the most?
- What is it that our company does that provides the most value to the customer?
- What is it that we do that is difficult for our competitors to imitate?

As you answer these questions, an idea of your company's primary product and competencies will begin to take shape. However, you and your team should be mindful that what might first seem to be critical to your company's success might turn out not to be that critical, and that is why the third question is extremely important. For example, a team defining core for Starbucks might say gourmet coffees is the product its customers know it for best, and serving a variety of coffee flavors provides the most value to the customer. But, a number of companies are known for their coffee and there are other coffee houses that serve a variety of made-to-order coffee drinks. So, what is it that Starbucks is truly known for? Its brand. Say the name "Starbucks" and just about anyone listening will see the Starbucks logo and picture the Starbucks located closest to them. Starbucks capitalizes on that brand recognition, using it to penetrate markets and boost sales.

To help ensure that you and your team are honing in on whether or not the business process is truly core, these are the next questions you should ask:

- Is there a service around what we believe is our core that contributes a great deal of value or exceeds the value of our primary product? Is it customer service? Delivery service? Value-added service?
- Would our primary product be the same if we didn't provide these services?
- Do our companies see this process as an important differentiator?

You and your team ask these questions to determine whether your company is better at making a product or servicing it. Suppose you are part of the core defining team at Domino's. Does Domino's make the best pizza on the market? Perhaps a few people think so, but the answer actually is "no." Is Domino's pizza the cheapest? No. So, what does Domino's do best? They can make a pizza in less than 8 minutes and deliver it in 45 minutes or less. If Domino's ever had to choose between making pizza that is featured in Gourmet magazine or making pizza fast and delivering it, I hope that it would choose the latter. In fact, Domino's could even offer this service to other pizza makers with better recipes who want to re-engineer the pizza-making process for faster service.

The core-defining team can further determine whether a physical product or a service is core by next asking:

- What percentage of the core cost of goods sold do these services make up?
- Do these services and the way they support our primary product align with our future goals for our organization?
- Would the individuals running these divisions ever run our company?
- Does/could the business they perform exist outside of our company? Is there an example of one outside of your company?

You and your core-defining team must be prepared to face some possibly difficult facts as you answer these questions. If you see that the services that support your product are eating into your profits and yet are not being done as well as they should, then perhaps they are not core functions, even if your company has been support-ing those services for generations. If your company's goal is to manufacture the best motherboards in the PC indus-try, perhaps delivering those motherboards to PC retailers faster than anyone else in the world is not aligned with that goal. Probably the most difficult of all the questions involves looking at who runs the business and identifying their contributions to the organization.

will help you evaluate what is core and what is not.[9]

---

[9] Charles Brunner, "Expanding Your World: Leveraging Core Competencies to Drive New Growth Opportunities," Product Genesis, Innovation Genesis, LLC, January 2006, pp. 6–7. http://www.productgenesis.com/archive/PG_Report_Expanding_Your_World_0601.pdf

A very useful exercise is to take the company's organizational chart and look at the leader of each operation and ask, "Could this person be CEO of this company one day?" Put a yes or no by their names, remembering that the answer should be based on that leader's function and not the leader's personality. If the answer is yes, that area is a candidate for primary core, and if the answer is no, then that might be a non-core function that can be outsourced. In the case of secondary core, the exercise is a little more difficult—separating primary and secondary core functions is not easy. The question to ask then is what kind of risk do you run by outsourcing this function.

The next step is to take the functions identified and determine if there is another company out there that has these functions as their primary core. Then, you and your team can ask if each person on the company's organizational chart could run those companies. If the answer is yes to both questions, you have identified a non-core function that could be outsourced.

Answering all the questions listed above for each business process will not be easy. But in the end, you and your team will have identified the organization's core competencies, as well as its non-core functions. At that point, you and your core-defining team can begin the process of identifying primary core competencies and secondary core competencies. This is where your answer or answers to, "What does our customer know us for most and how do we best touch the customer?" are important. Perhaps your customers know you best for your brand. Or maybe your customers recognize your company as the one that developed a life-saving drug or made it easier for them to ship packages. Your primary core competencies are going to be those your customer perceives as differentiating you from your competitors.

Your secondary core competencies are more likely to be found in the answer to, "What do we do that brings the most value to the customer?" In other words, your customers might not know everything you do to make their experiences all they expect or more, but if these things are not done well, you will lose them. Imagine a customer's reaction if the motherboard died on a Dell computer he had purchased a few days earlier. Customers rarely say, "Yeah, I buy Dell computers because their motherboards are the best in the business," but if all of a sudden Dell motherboards crashed within days of a purchase, well, Dell wouldn't be in business much longer. You might also want to ask yourself "What do I risk if I try to outsource this function?" If you determine that there is a small risk, but that it is worth taking for the sake of improving other functions, then you have most likely identified a secondary core function.

Identifying primary and secondary core functions is critical to deciding what functions to keep in-house and what to outsource. There are those who will wonder why that is so. Surely, this is a no-brainer, and only non-core functions should be outsourced while all core functions should be kept in-house, right? The answer to this question can sometimes be yes, but in many cases, it might be no. Your company might compete better in the marketplace if it outsources a secondary core function or if it keeps a primary non-core function or functions in-house. That is why the distinctions between primary core and secondary core are so important. Once you have made them, you are ready to begin the process of evaluating functions and reaching a consensus about which processes will be kept in-house and which will be done by other organizations.

Before you begin the evaluation process, it is important to realize that this can be even more difficult than defining core because word will soon be out that functions will be outsourced. People will become secretive and resentful because they are fearful of losing their jobs. While being laid off is only one of the three staffing outcomes of outsourcing—the other two are transfers to the service provider and redeployment elsewhere in the organization—layoffs after outsourcing make the most press.

Corporate America doesn't help; in April 2004 an article in *USA Today* reported that, in some companies, American employees losing their jobs to India had to train their replacements before leaving the company. Therefore, it cannot be stressed enough how important correct, consistent and timely communication to the right people is. Keeping staff informed through regular communication and monitoring overall morale go a long way toward easing fear, doubt, and uncertainty as you begin the business process evaluation process. This is in keeping with your role as an inspirational leader.

The first step in evaluating business processes for outsourcing is identifying which processes need strategic outsourcing and which should be contracted. Strategic outsourcing, which is what is meant in this book by "outsourcing," involves working with one or more service providers to bring about a significant improvement in business performance. Strategic outsourcing is best suited to secondary core and primary non-core functions, and it is only likely to bring the desired results if management is prepared to adopt a completely new perspective on management control. The Core Competency Matrix can help you in this process (Figure 4).

|  | **Primary Focus** | **Secondary Focus** |
|---|---|---|
| **Core Process** | Insource | Insource<br>Outsource |
| **Non-Core Process** | Insource<br>Outsource<br>Contract | Outsource<br>Contract |

FIGURE 4. CORE COMPETENCY MATRIX.

Strategic outsourcing is quite different from contracting, which basically delegates the responsibility to an organization, and then lets them get on with it. The organization involved will have no real interest in your company once its own responsibilities have been fulfilled. For example, the process of hiring a landscaping company to take care of the grounds is a very good example of contracting which is best suited to secondary non-core functions (although there can be secondary non-core functions that warrant strategic outsourcing).

Making these determinations is critical in understanding the possible benefits from performing the outsourcing. Once you have defined your primary core processes, you will have a list of other functions and activities, some of which might be immediately recognized as possible outsourcing targets and others that may need further evaluation. From this point, you can develop a baseline for objective decision-making, define the business processes and their value, and recognize what non-core functions contribute to your business and which simply help support your physical plant and employees.

## Defining Core Outsourcing Targets

Determining the functions and segments in which outsourcing will have the most value is a critical part of the process. A look at almost any company's history shows the deterioration in performance that occurs when company leaders and management "take their eyes off the ball" and begin to focus on non-core activities. Eventually, their profit performance and competitiveness decline. Companies must focus management time and attention on their core competencies and maintain efforts to continuously improve those functions that are core. Therefore, functions that are outside of the primary core (and that can include secondary core) should be outsourced to free management time and organizational resources to work on the highest priority activities—primary core competencies.

No outsourcing strategy should be rushed into without careful evaluation and analysis. You need to learn about internal process needs and service requirements for the functions or processes and understand the cost structure of the functions or processes that are candidates for outsourcing; otherwise, the outsourcing strategy will become yet one more non-core competency that demands considerable time and focus from management and leadership. Then, you must find qualified providers to meet the service and cost needs of the company. This section discusses the internal baseline analysis and market research required to select a specific function or process for outsourcing and then describes the process of making recommendations for outsourcing.

*Baselining and Market Research*

One of the common mistakes companies make once they have decided to outsource is to rush through or gloss over the baselining step in their eagerness to get started. However, this can have serious consequences and might adversely affect the future of the company because it will result in:

• Poor outsourcing selection decisions.

• Inadequate performance measurements (which will cause poor performance).

• A rise in costs until they are higher than the current in-house function or process.

There must be a clear understanding of the economic and practical feasibility of outsourcing and the market capability to effectively provide the needed service. Your company should not outsource to avoid an existing problem or rush into outsourcing because it appears to be the way to bypass poor performance. Your impetus for outsourcing should be to accomplish positive goals and not to avoid negative circumstances. Outsourcing an ineffective function or process is not a guarantee that the function or process will work any better or be any less costly than what is being done today. That is why baselining is so important—it requires a company to examine all aspects of their processes and functions before any rash decisions can be made.

A baselining and market research initiative has five basic components. They are:

1. **Establishing a Baseline Analysis Team:** Performing a baseline analysis and market research is a methodical process that should be conducted carefully and thoroughly. Therefore, the first thing a baselining and market research initiative needs is people to perform the tasks associated with it. Any company that has decided to outsource must establish a Baseline Analysis Team to oversee the evaluation processes. This team is created by an executive steering team that identifies the team leader and team members to complete the baseline from available internal resources. Ideally, the baseline analysis team should be comprised of those with insider knowledge of your company and one or two outsiders who know the business but have nothing to protect.

2. **Defining data requirements and analysis methodology:** This definition process starts with the development of a list of the data required to fully document each current function or process, including the following:

   • Documentation of the scope of the function or process considered for outsourcing.

   • Key function or process inputs through the development of process flow diagrams.

   • Equipment and facilities required by the function or process.

   • Staffing levels for peak and routine demand levels.

   • A breakdown of the total cost of operations.

   • Quality requirements.

   • Measures of performance.

   • Service level and delivery requirements.

   Each of these pieces is a part of the outsourcing decision because you use them to determine the health, effectiveness, efficiency, quality and cost structure of each business function.

# Preparing and Evaluating RFIs for Market Research of Available Providers

The RFI you prepare for your market research should be detailed enough to allow a high-level due diligence of available providers. The information the respondents should provide includes:

- Company strengths and weaknesses
- Relevant previous experience, such as a client list
- Reference sites for similar outsourcing
- Financial stability and growth plans
- Availability of knowledgeable technical resources
- Responsiveness and interest in the business
- Indications of company culture, such as values, employee expectations, goals, and objective

To evaluate the RFI responses to identify potential service providers, use the following selection criteria:

- Technical ability-Do the people performing the work have up-to-date knowledge and training on the technology necessary for the job? Can they provide the level of technical services and compatibility required for the job?
- Depth of experience in the field-How long has the company been performing its

*Continues on next page*

3. **Developing a baseline model:** To validate existing functional processes, develop a baseline model by following these steps:

   a) Collect and analyze the data for each outsourcing candidate. This includes function and process operational data; organizational structure; finance budgets and cost data; inventory of assets; and outputs and metrics used to measure service level performance.

   b) Map internal business processes. Document information flows, business rules, and so on and determines whether they meet business and mission-critical goals. This activity helps the team identify functional gaps, out-dated methodology, and organizational issues.

   c) Develop the internal cost and service level baselines.

   These baseline summary activities and the summary documents you create throughout this process are the key to deciding what functions to outsource and what to keep in-house. Take note: This is not the time to protect interests or gloss over failures. At the same time, processes that are done well should also be given their due.

4. **Performing market evaluation of service providers:** It might seem premature to identify and evaluate service providers during this stage of the process. After all, your company is not sure what it's going to outsource yet. However, the availability and quality of those offering services for functions that may be outsourced has a direct impact on whether it is feasible to outsource a function or not. For example, if no one out there has the capability to handle the function that you are considering outsourcing, then you should probably keep that function in house, at least for the time being. Market research also adds weight to a team's outsourcing recommendation and makes the decision of whether or not to outsource easier. To begin the market research process:

a) Identify potential providers of the service or function, using your industry knowledge, networking, the Web and other outside resources.

b) Prepare a request for information (RFI) that you can use to solicit a number of potential vendors for information about their products and services.

c) Evaluate the RFI responses to see who might be the best fit for your outsourcing initiative.

After each business segment has its own baseline summary document and the market research is complete, it is time to make outsourcing recommendations.

*Making Outsourcing Recommendations*

Before you make outsourcing recommendations, you and your company should revisit your goals, mission, strategic vision, and requirements.[26] Also, look for what it will take to make sure that your primary core functions get the attention they deserve from leadership and management. After you have completed these tasks, follow these steps:

1. Identify those functions or processes that meet company financial return objectives. Everyone involved in the process should be able to agree whether the following statements are "True" or "False" for each function:

   • This function isn't central to generating profits or competitive success.

   • This function is a routine one that wastes valuable time and energy.

   • This function is either temporary or it recurs in cycles.

   • It's less expensive to have someone else handle this segment of business than it is to do it in-house.

services? How many clients has it had? Are site visits encouraged?

• Company and organizational culture-Does the provider have an organizational culture committed to continuous improvement? What are its goals, vision and mission? Are its employees aligned with these? Does it have an approach and philosophy consistent with yours?

• Financial stability-What are the company's finances like? Are they a well-established company with the means to take on your company's job?

Not only will these criteria help your company gain a greater understanding of the services offered by outsourcing providers and the market for specific services overall, but they will be useful when you are at the request for proposal (RFP) stage in your company's outsourcing initiative. Once all the evaluations have been prepared, they will become part of the process of developing specific outsourcing recommendations.

---

[26] For more information about goals, mission, strategic vision, and requirements, see Jim A. Tompkins, *Revolution: Take Charge Strategies for Business Success* (Raleigh, NC, 1998) and James A. Tompkins, *Logistics and Manufacturing Outsourcing: Harness Your Core Competencies* (Raleigh, NC, 2005).

- This function can be done cheaper in-house, but it drains resources that could be better used elsewhere.
- The skill(s) required for this function are so specialized that it is impractical to have regular staff do it.

Those functions that earn a "false" probably should remain in-house. Those that earn a "True" are most likely to be good candidates for outsourcing. This exercise will lead to judicious outsourcing recommendations that will allow your company to get where it wants to be. You will know the potential savings, in terms of time and money, as well as potential returns on investment. You will have assessed what you can do within your company and what you can't.

2. Prioritize the list of potential outsource candidates created while the team was conducting its market research. Take a critical look at the evaluations you made based on the RFIs you received and try to determine which candidates best met the evaluation criteria. You may want to devise a scoring or rating technique of some sort or decide which criteria carry more weight.

3. After the list of candidates is prioritized, obtain consensus on the prioritized list.

At this point, you will have identified your outsourcing targets. You can then develop a schedule and plan for the outsourcing process, which is discussed in detail in the next chapter.

## On the Elevator

Outsourcing is a management tool that shifts the organizational structure of companies. It is a business transformation process that is a key component in the process of becoming a bold organization and can create great opportunity for improved performance. When done properly, outsourcing primary non-core operations functions yields numerous benefits—benefits with direct impact on a company, such as:

- Focus on core competency
- Reduction in manufacturing and distribution costs
- Reduction in management and hourly head count
- Improved accuracy
- Flexibility and wider range of service
- Access to global networks and superior technology
- Improved service
- Improved quality
- Reduction in capital investment and cash infusion

The key to taking advantage of all outsourcing has to offer lies in your outsourcing strategy—defining your core competencies, defining targets, and managing your outsourcing relationships.

# Chapter 6: DEFINING CORE COMPETENCIES AND OUTSOURCING TARGETS

The process of defining core requires awareness of the four types of business functions within a company—primary core, secondary core, primary non-core, and secondary non-core. Primary core functions are the things that differentiate your company in the marketplace and more, importantly, they are the reason your customers come to you. Secondary core functions are those things that bring value to your customer and must be done well, but at the same time are not visible to your customer. Primary non-core functions are those that can affect your relationship with your customer but are not what your business is about. Secondary non-core functions are those processes that are necessary for running it but do not affect your company's success.

There are some definite questions that must be asked in order to understand and evaluate core. They are:

- Who are our customers?
- How do the functions we have defined touch the customer? Or do they touch the customer?
- What is it that our customers know us for most?
- What is it that our company does that provides the most value to the customer?
- What is it that we do that may be difficult for our competitors to imitate?
- Would the individuals running these divisions ever run our company? Does or could the business they perform exist outside of our company? Is there an example of one outside of our company?

Answering all of these questions for each of the business processes you have defined will help you understand if they are a good target for evaluation. Once you have defined core and its supporting processes, there needs to be consensus around which to evaluate outsourcing.

To select specific functions for outsourcing, an internal baseline analysis and market research is required for each specific function to determine whether it should be selected for outsourcing. A baselining and market research initiative has five basic components. They are:

- Establishing a Baseline Analysis Team
- Defining data requirements and analysis methodology
- Developing a baseline model
- Performing market evaluation of service providers

After the baselining and market research initiative is complete, you and your outsourcing team can determine the feasibility of outsourcing specific functions or processes based on the work it has done, identify those functions or processes that meet company financial return objectives, prioritize the list of potential outsource candidates, obtain consensus on the prioritized list, and prepare for the next steps in the outsourcing process.

# Chapter 7
# FINDING THE RIGHT OUTSOURCING PROVIDER

"Ultimately, outsourcing is about people. More often than not, outsourcing initiatives with high success rates involve two companies whose cultures mesh."

After you have identified primary and secondary core processes and determined your outsourcing targets, it is time to solicit providers for the process or processes being outsourced. The solicitation process involves more than writing an RFP, however. It is actually a combination of six steps:

1. Setting realistic expectations
2. Setting goals and a timeline
3. Developing the list of potential providers
4. Evaluating the responses to the RFI
5. Developing a scope of work
6. Drafting the RFP itself

After that, you can send the RFP out and prepare your company to evaluate the proposals you will receive.

Choosing the best service provider is an obvious key to success in an outsourcing initiative. Because of the impact outsourcing has on a company's bottom line, you must have a methodical bid evaluation and provider selection process, one that should not be rushed even when there are time constraints or there is pressure to make a decision quickly. The selection process can be time consuming and costly, but the good news is that there are time-tested methodologies that can help you make the right decision.

The process begins with short-listing, and final selection follows. Once the selection is made, the legal relationship begins; however, you must involve your legal team in the selection process, especially after you have determined your short list. Another important factor in the process is cultural fit, which is often not considered part of the evaluation criteria. This is a mistake, because it has been proven that when the cultures of two

# Understanding Goals is the Most Important Factor in Outsourcing Success: Survey

In 2004, Enterprise Systems conducted an outsourcing survey. More than 700 organizations participated. Respondents came from various industries, including advertising, aerospace, financial services, manufacturing retail, and telecommunications. Nearly 29 percent of respondents identified themselves as directors, CIOs and CEOs; another 22 percent were managers; and 49 percent were IT staff, coordinators or consultants. More than 71 percent of respondents said they have been directly involved in some aspect of their company's outsourcing efforts in the previous year. Slightly more-72.4 percent-anticipated being involved in the next year.

One of the survey questions asked the respondents, what, in their experience, is the most important factor in successful outsourcing projects? The results are shown in the table below.

*Continues on next page*

companies clash the outsourcing process becomes an uphill battle that typically starts on day one and ends in termination or even litigation.

This chapter describes the six steps involved in the solicitation process, and then focuses on creating the short list, the final evaluation, cultural fit, and the post-selection process.

## Setting Realistic Expectations

The process of setting expectations for outsourcing should start with an examination of what outsourcing should accomplish and what it shouldn't. If your company is considering using a 3PL, for example, it is important for you and your team to understand that 3PL is the use of an outside firm to perform some or all of the supply chain functions an organization requires. This can involve any aspect of logistics and is more than simply outsourcing warehousing or transportation. As a rule, a 3PL service provider integrates more than one link within the overall supply chain, but the service can be as narrow or broad as needed. Therefore, the company should learn all it can about the different types of 3PLs and what they can offer. Otherwise, it will not be possible to develop an RFP with the correct elements. This applies to any kind of outsourcing provider, not just 3PL.

Also, you and your company must understand that you might have to overhaul internal processes that are not being outsourced as part of the initiative if you truly want to improve your supply chain. Similar research and education is necessary before developing an RFP for outsourcing manufacturing processes. Therefore, some helpful questions to ask at this point are:

- Has the business case been well defined?
- What if we do nothing?
- What are the benefits of outsourcing? Does it fit into our short- and long-term business strategies?
- What are the risks?
- Have all the stake holders been identified?
- What are the required resources?

Asking these questions forces everyone in the company to take an inventory of emotions. Answering them allows realistic expectations to be set before any commitments are made. It also allows the team to set realistic goals and timelines, which is the next step in the RFP process.

## Setting Goals and a Timeline

After everyone understands what outsourcing is and management is on board, you and your team can clearly set forth the goals you want the service provider to help you achieve. While you are identifying these goals, make sure that you are focused on the positive. Poor performance should not be the driving force behind an outsourcing plan. Remember, the most important goal for outsourcing is to return your focus to the levels necessary for peak performance. Examples of other positive goals include:

- Increased customer satisfaction
- Access to world-class technology
- Increased competitiveness
- Cost reduction
- Release of capital
- Reduce future investment
- Reduce risk

These goals must fit the organization's needs over the life of the relationship. At this point, you must not assume that today's level of performance is what is required for the service provider.

Once your goals are in place, you and your team should develop a detailed, realistic timeline for the outsource process. The critical task here is to identify key dates for:

- RFI release, response deadline, and list of RFP recipients
- RFP release and response deadline
- Site visits
- Short list
- Due diligence
- Selection

| | |
|---|---|
| Understanding the goals | 27.8 percent |
| Selecting the right vendor | 24.5 percent |
| On-going management | 19.9 percent |
| A properly structured contract | 12.5 percent |
| Strategic vision | 7.1 percent |
| No previous experience | 3.7 percent |
| Other | 2.5 percent |

TABLE 1. SUCCESS FACTORS.

As you can see, understanding the goals was considered the factor that is most critical to outsourcing success.[p]

[p] "Outsourcing Survey, Part 1: Who and Where?" Enterprise Systems News, 14 Oct. 2004, http://esj.com/enterprise/article.aspx?EditorialsID=1144

- Term sheet signing
- Contract signing
- Implementation

Once you have clearly identified your outsourcing goals and created a realistic time-line, you can develop a list of potential providers and decide which of them will receive your RFP.

## Developing the List of Potential Providers

The process of developing a list of potential providers actually begins when your company conducts the market research of companies that offer services correlating with the process you have targeted for outsourcing as discussed in Chapter 6. At that time, you should research companies that offer services that correlate with the targeted pro-cesses. Now that your company has identified the processes to be outsourced, you can take that research and use it to compile an initial list of candidates. Also, you can ask for more suggestions. Some other sources for candidates include industry magazines, the internet, other companies that have outsourced the same function and networks devel-oped over time.

Ideally, the number of candidates on the list should be between eight and twelve, and it should represent a cross-section of service providers—regional, national, global, privately held, publicly held, established and start-ups (new growth).

The next step is to identify the capabilities of each company on your list. One of the best ways to accomplish this is to make an initial call and talk about timelines, your process, and initial expectations. Ask them if they know your specific industry. If you are a small customer, ask them if they have provided services for small companies in the past and if they continue to do so. You probably do not want to send an RFP to a company that has only done business with Fortune 500 companies or a company that tried to work with a small customer but was not successful. If you are a big company, the inverse applies.

Your company should also not limit its list to outsource providers only; there may be industry players who can meet your requirements that are not necessarily considered outsourcers. You want to consider all viable candidates. Once you have done this, you can prepare an RFI. If you developed one as part of the process of identifying outsourc-ing targets, you may use it as a framework. The one you develop in this case, however, will be more specific.

## The RFI

RFIs (Requests for Information) come in many shapes and sizes. There are numerous approaches and formats. The structure we find most successful includes the following:

- An introductory letter that states the goal of the outsource initiative and instructions for responding to the RFI,
- 'Intent to respond' notice that serves as a confidentiality agreement and includes the date of receipt, the company's name, their contacts, the areas in the RFI that the client intends to answer and a signature,
- Description of your evaluation process that states the key decision criteria and your timeframes, guidelines and contacts, the purpose and scope of the RFI and your business requirements; and
- RFI questionnaire that asks the respondents to provide information about their company, asks about approach and capabilities on functional specifics (based on a description of what you are outsourcing), requests sample metrics and inquires about the provider's competitive differences or advantages. If applicable, this questionnaire should also ask about the company's technology applications and their capabilities as well as service levels.

## Evaluating the Responses to the RFI

After you have prepared the RFI, send it to the candidates you selected earlier. When all the responses are returned, you have several methods you can use to draw up a list of qualified respondents that should receive your RFP. One option is to use the evaluation criteria section in the RFI as a guideline. Another option is to create a scoring matrix. A third option is to create a summary of each response to your RFI that addresses the following topics:

- Capability
- Philosophy
- Financial data
- Service

The RFI summary is an excellent "weeding out process" because it levels the respondents' playing field, and it helps you zero in on key issues and qualities. It is also an excellent tool for directing senior management focus on only qualified providers because it provides a granular level of information quickly.[27]

---

[27] For more details about the RFI and what should be in it, see James A. Tompkins, Ph.D., Steven W. Simonson, Bruce W. Tompkins, and Brian E. Upchurch, *Logistics and Manufacturing Outsourcing: Harness Your Core Competencies* (Raleigh, NC: 2005), pp. 75-77. Available at www.tompkinsinc.com.

After you have applied your evaluation methodology or methodologies, you will have a solid list of companies to receive the RFP. Your next step is to draft a scope of work.

### Developing a Scope of Work

You use an RFP to communicate your expectations to potential service providers. However, before you draft the RFP, your company must first identify these expectations. You do that by developing a scope of work, which should have the following:

- A description of the nature of the process
- Operational data and current process maps (base data with growth potential and a description of current or desired processes—if the processes do not currently exist—so that potential providers can understand the magnitude of the volume and the amount of effort required to process the effort)
- Detailed reporting requirements
- What tasks are to be performed
- Expected growth and change in business in the future
- The level of performance desired
- A list of all the external factors that affect the process

You should also include the costs of performing the work, and any fee structure agreed upon should be spelled out. You must clearly state hours and days of operations, and include any special services that do not fall under the normal schedule. Once the scope is defined, the team should make sure that the boundaries of what is to be outsourced are clearly established.

The scope of work must include input from the people currently involved in the process that will be outsourced, and processes within the company that are not part of the process but that the process touches. We also recommend that your company consult with an outside resource that is experienced in outsourcing that process. Combining these different points of view is the best way to deal with the problem of vested knowledge vs. objectivity as you create the scope of work. Having an external resource involved in this process removes emotional ties and bias, adds professionalism and keeps participants focused on execution. Without this objectivity, there is the danger of duplicating existing poor processes in the scope of work and reinventing the wheel.

### Drafting the RFP

Once you have developed the scope of work, you have the framework for the RFP, which is one of the most critical components of the outsourcing process. A good RFP is the foundation for a successful outsourcing venture. Surprisingly, many companies do not seem to realize this. Often they approach drafting the RFP with less care than writing an email, and the result is that many poorly developed and written RFPs have been dissemiated over the years, resulting in frustrations and failed outsourcing ventures. I have seen instances where someone in a company develops a one-page scope of work, hands that over to a potential provider, and asks them to bid on a critical element of work.

The RFP spells out your requirements for service (including the scope of work), but also it gives prospective service providers the information they need to prepare a bid.

It is the template for a provider's contract with a company, and if the provider does not know what the company contracting with them expects, a long contract negotiation is a certainty. Both parties might end up pushing away from the table and deciding that it's not worth the effort to do business together. Therefore, an RFP should provide potential providers with a clear set of requirements, a clear path forward and a clear desire for innovation and creativity. It does not tell candidates how to do their jobs; instead, it informs them of what needs to be done. It sets forth a company's full range of requirements to include slow, typical and high levels of requirements.

A good RFP has the following structure:

- Introduction: This is a high-level section that identifies the services to be outsourced, states objectives, provides an overview of what is in the RFP while introducing what is out of scope and touches on bid options and different scenarios.
- Scope of work: This is the scope of work discussed in the previous section. It should also include a concise history of your company and your business requirements.
- Instructions to bidder: This part of the RFP tells bidders your company's intentions, the timetables involved and how to submit bids, including how many copies of their proposal you wish to receive and a copy of a proposal pricing form. It should describe correspondence control, how you plan to receive and answer questions from the bidders, and what you require in the way of responses, including format.
- Company information: In this section, you request that bidders provide evidence that they can meet your requirements, including a statement of their capabilities, financial statements, client references, project descriptions or case studies and resumes of members of their management and proposed project implementation teams.
- Account management: This section describes how you will manage their account and sets forth your reporting requirements, how the account will be serviced (including an escalation path for problems), strategic relationships, the project schedule and pricing and access to any online communications and documentation libraries.
- Performance expected during due diligence and site visits: Providers must know that they will be asked to show an existing process in their company that is close to the process being outsourced.
- Terms and conditions: These are your standard terms and conditions that serve as a template for a future contract.
- Evaluation criteria: In this section, you inform bidders of those factors that will

drive your choice of provider, including cost, their ability to meet established metrics, their experience, their strengths and the accuracy and completeness of their response to the RFP.

• Documentation to be included: This section can include more detailed resumes, annual reports, financial statements and any other evidence you request (such as autoCAD layouts or evidence of design work or system design if applicable).

The most important thing to remember when you draft an RFP is that it must be clear, comprehensive and honest. Share as much information as you can. That is the only way you will receive clear, comprehensive and honest proposals in return. An outsourcing venture is doomed from the outset if the customer and vendor are still discovering information about each other during the term of the contract. This will happen if you are not up front in the very beginning.

After your outsourcing team has drafted the RFP, the next move is simple: send the RFP to the list of potential providers you identified when you evaluated the responses to the RFIs. After you have received all the responses by the deadline you specified, you're ready to create your short list.

## The Short List

Creating the short list requires some effort and might involve reading the proposals several times. Tompkins Associates uses and recommends the following process:

1. Check all the proposals to see if they address the full scope of the functions to be outsourced and make sure there are names and numbers for credit references and clients. Incomplete proposals can then be eliminated before serious work begins.

2. Review the proposals to search for viable candidates. You might wish to draw up a list of questions about the proposals, such as:

    • Does the proposal demonstrate familiarity with your industry? Or does it use a lot of buzzwords to imply knowledge that the company really does not have?

    • Does the proposal demonstrate the company's financial stability? Or are financials glossed over in an attempt to disguise problems?

    • Does the proposal demonstrate that the company provides the appropriate services necessary for your outsourcing initiatives? Or does it try to sell other services because it is better qualified to handle those?

    • Does the proposal demonstrate that the provider is organized in its approach to a project? Or is the company "all over the map" in its description of processes?

    • Are the proposal's terms and conditions clear, fair and appropriate? Or will it take the efforts of a legal team similar to that representing a defendant in a corporate accounting scandal to unravel them?

3. Check references. Call the respondents' customers to gain insights into each candidate's performance. A good way to do this is to use the same evaluation criteria used to create an RFI summary, and ask the customers to comment on each. Also, it's a good idea to ask each reference to give one example or more of how the provider recovered from a difficult situation, such as poor service levels.

There are other actions you can take that complement and supplement the proposal review. These activities include:

• Face-to-face meetings: Invite respondents to visit your company and make oral presentations.

• Operations site visits: Touring each candidate's facilities can help you determine if they are viable providers whose culture fits with yours (discussed in more detail in a later section), especially if you feel you've been dazzled by a powerful sales presentation during the face-to-face meetings.

• Post-proposal communications review: Examine each candidate's responses to your questions and other communications about their proposals. In large firms, proposals are often subjected to a thorough internal editorial review before they are sent out. Many times those doing the work may contribute some information to it, but professional communicators package it. It is important to see how candidates think "on the fly" and to determine how well the actual people doing the work will interact with your company should they be selected.

Throughout the proposal review and the activities surrounding it, you and your team should be comparing companies to one another and taking detailed notes, not just on the companies but on the members' own responses to the proposals. Ask specific, clear questions of yourselves and the respondents. Be sure that those members of the team that paid visits to potential provider sites have documented their experiences completely. It may take some time, many meetings, and perhaps a few headaches, but in the end, you will have arrived at a short list of contenders, and the rigorous evaluation of the finalists to determine which will get the project can begin.

## Final Evaluation

Contrary to popular belief, deciding which of the providers on your short list will be your outsourcer involves more than contacting the provider with the lowest bid and beginning the contract negotiation process. Although cost is an important factor in your decision and it is a key differentiator if you have two equally qualified candidates, it must not be the only one. Instead, you must develop a list of weighted criteria (one that includes cost) and rank each element.

# Evaluation Criteria Yield Surprising Results: Mallinckrodt and MedTech

Mallinckrodt Critical Care Division, Inc. of Irvine, California, sent an RFP worldwide to selected medical products manufacturers to redesign and manufacture a new generation of products that met specifications for the international marketplace. The MedTech Group, Inc. of New Jersey was one of them. During the selection process, MedTech was considered to be at a disadvantage, because their manufacturing operations were in New Jersey, across the country from the California plant where Mallinckrodt had to sterilize the final product. Further, MedTech was viewed as having no experience molding this particular type of product. In fact, other Mallinckrodt manufacturing sites were also included in this search. Despite the perceived disadvantages, MedTech was awarded the program based on Mallinckrodt's unique decision-making process.

According to Tony Wondka, Project Manager at Mallinckrodt, one of the reasons MedTech came out on top was because MedTech showed the most knowledge and understanding of what they truly needed. The rating system used to make the decision

*Continues on next page*

There are many different criteria you can use in your final evaluation. Which ones you use and how you will weight them depends on the end objectives of the project and what is important to your company. The size of your project will also determine the weight assigned to your criteria. There are, however, certain criteria that should be included and weighted in your final evaluation, no matter what your project. Some examples of the criteria are:

- Financial stability—does the candidate have excellent credit and bank references? Does it have a solid financial statement?
- Service offerings—does the candidate provide the services detailed in the functional requirements portion of the RFP?
- Culture—does the candidate share your philosophy and values? Are its mission and strategic goals in line with yours?
- Customer satisfaction—what have customers said about their relationships with the candidate? Will the candidate seek and use input from your customers to improve the level of service? Will the candidate be able to maintain and exceed current levels of service?
- Operations—does the candidate use the appropriate methods, resources and processes to assure operational efficiency and effectiveness? Does it have procedures in place that protect against equipment breakdown and malfunction? How does the candidate assure continuous improvement? If the outsourcing process requires using the candidate's facility or facilities, what is the availability and location of critical areas (for example, usable warehouse space, dock capacity, lighting and so forth)?
- Technology—does the candidate use technology effectively to operate its business? Does it have access to the world-class technology you would use if you were keeping the process in-house? Is the candidate committed to investing in new technologies that can improve processes?

- Cost—does the candidate's bid cover all requested items with the necessary degree of detail? Will the candidate make an acceptable profit? How does the bid compare with others of equal capability?
- Flexibility—does the potential provider operate its company so it can change with your needs and the needs of your customers? Is the candidate willing to make adjustments? If you have to make significant changes, will the candidate be able to respond?
- Systems—do the candidate's information systems enable the sharing of a variety of information securely? Does the candidate possess or can it develop, install and operate the same or better information systems than you currently use? What will it take to integrate its systems with yours?

Once you have identified your criteria, you apply it to each candidate. It is often helpful to create a matrix or scoreboard to use in your final evaluation. All selection team members must rate the short-listed proposals against the standards. Performance categories should be listed and rated on a scale of one to five, with five being the highest.

An example of an assessment method that can help you with the final evaluation is shown in the table below. It features suggested performance categories and weightings.

included experience in assembly, insert molding and packaging, production costs, delivery of product once in production and the ability to meet schedule requirements and logistics.

Concerns regarding a distance factor were quickly resolved with MedTech's ability to communicate electronically with Mallinckrodt's engineers. And MedTech's lack of experience producing similar products was quickly overcome by personal visits to the Mallinckrodt site. Ultimately, Mallinckrodt's training of MedTech's operators in building these units ensured consistency between the two companies.[q]

---

[q] The MedTech Group, Inc. "Success Stories—New Product Development: Redesign and Manufacture of New Generation Product," http://www.medtech-grp.com/site/home.nsf/e_Index/successstory2

| Category | Category Rating | Weight | Category Score | Target Score |
|---|---|---|---|---|
| Financial Stability | 5 | 15 | 75 | 75 |
| Service Offerings | 4 | 15 | 60 | 75 |
| Culture | 4 | 15 | 60 | 75 |
| Customer Satisfaction | 3 | 15 | 45 | 75 |
| Operations | 3 | 10 | 30 | 50 |
| Technology | 4 | 10 | 40 | 50 |
| Cost | 2 | 10 | 20 | 50 |
| Flexibility | 3 | 5 | 15 | 25 |
| Control Systems | 5 | 5 | 25 | 25 |
| Total | | | 370 (74%) | 500 |

TABLE 2. SUGGESTED PERFORMANCE CATEGORIES AND WEIGHTINGS.

## Cultural Fit: A Real-World Example

Tompkins Associates recently worked with a client who went through a very strenuous selection process for outsourcing their distribution processes. Because of a bad past experience, the client had a perception that large global distribution providers would prove to be cold and uninterested in their business. However, we encouraged them to use a global provider, and, in the end, the client was absolutely surprised. Their people were knowledgeable and professional, winning "hands down" on culture. What the client experienced was the value of a global provider with a strong regional feel.

Then, several months later, we had the opportunity to represent another client with similar outsource requirements but in another geographic region. As a result of the success with the previous client, we invited the provider to bid on the RFP. The result was a disappointment. Although it was the same company, with the same process, and the same pitch, the differences between the client's approach and the provider's approach were too great. This was a well-learned lesson not soon forgotten.

Depending on the goals of the outsourcing initiative, weighting can vary from project to project. Ratings are based on qualitative and quantitative assessments. Each category should then be rated to reflect its relative importance. The total of all weights is 100, which yields a maximum score of 500 points. There will be situations that cause the realistic maximum rating for each category to be less than five, so a target rating is assigned to each category.

The category rating and target rating are multiplied by the category weight to obtain a category score and a target score. The total category score is then divided by the total target score to obtain a performance index. The highest performance index indicates the best candidate and, by default, the provider you have selected for your outsourcing initiative.

This type of activity might appear complex and difficult, but it is vital to the evaluation and selection process because it provides the clearest picture of each candidate's capabilities. Without that picture, there is the possibility that you will make a selection that could be devastating to your organization. Using this assessment method is the best way to assure that there is a good fit between you and your provider, one that most likely will lead to a harmonious, beneficial relationship.

### Cultural Fit

In the evaluation process, how the potential provider's company culture stands up against yours is important because, ultimately, outsourcing is about people. More often than not, outsourcing initiatives with high success rates involve two companies whose cultures mesh. When there is a solid cultural fit between an outsourcer and a service provider, communication flows, and challenges are met and overcome.

At the same time, cultural fit can be difficult to measure and certainly objective. Some examples of things to consider regarding a provider's culture while you are evaluating their bid include:

- Do they share your values? Do they approach quality, cost position, human resources, and the community the same way your company does?
- Are they open with you when they answer your questions?
- Is working with them easy for you?
- Are their interactions natural rather than forced?
- Do they genuinely appear to want the opportunity? Are they excited and enthusiastic about the possibility of working with your company?

While you determine the answers to these questions, you must keep in mind the fact that often a potential provider's "front men" share your cultural values, but the entire organization does not. To determine whether the organization shares them at all levels, you should incorporate a company culture investigation into your site visit by making sure, when you are touring a potential provider's facilities or observing their processes, that you have access to the people doing the actual work. Take some time and ask the workers questions and gauge their reactions. Are they enthusiastic and helpful? Do they seem to enjoy what they're doing? Do they demonstrate substantial knowledge of the processes or facility you are observing? Are they experts or do they demonstrate a high degree of experience?

By combining your experiences in face-to-face meetings with company leaders and talking to workers on the floor during site visits, you will have multiple points for determining whether the company's culture fits with yours. If the workers project ideas and attitudes similar to those of its leaders and sales team and they are in line with yours, most likely you will have a solid contender for your final selection.

## Post-Selection

It is important to remember that a potential provider responding to a medium to large outsourcing initiative can spend upwards of $75,000. Therefore, after you have made your selection, don't forget to thank the participants that did not make the short list and notify them that finalists have been chosen. In the excitement of having chosen a provider and the flurry that surrounds the beginning of the new relationship and the contract negotiations, this courtesy is often forgotten.

When you thank the respondents, we recommend that you share with each why they were not the best match this time out. It is very frustrating for a provider to learn that it has not been selected for a project without being told who was or why a different selection is made. Being open and honest with them, but with tact and diplomacy, can ease frustrations, and your input is likely to help them as they prepare to respond to other RFPs. Ending the selection process on a good note will also benefit your company because you never know when you might run across the provider again or even require their services at some point in the future.

## The Evaluation Process: Additional Tips

Here are some additional tips that can help you with your selection process:

Control communications during the evaluation process by assigning a single point of contact to communicate with the potential providers. Give all providers the same information.

The evaluation process is a business decision, not only a low-cost decision or a personal preference. The process must be methodical. Relationships and executive preferences should not be overly emphasized. The evaluation criteria must be rigorously applied in a fair and equitable manner.

The evaluation process should not be rushed. Often time pressures are present, but these pressures should not result in allowing the process to be anything other than fair, detailed and robust.

Have a clear understanding of how your team will be handling short list determination, second visits and additional information requests. Be sure the short list process is followed and the evaluation team and process are maintained through the short list and ultimate selection process.

Be sure to evaluate proposals and not sales presentations. The written bid is what should be evaluated. In a similar way,

*Continues on next page*

At the same time, you should not tell any potential provider they are "the winner" until after a binding term sheet or contract is signed. Until a binding relationship is established, you should always retain more than one option. In fact, for large outsourcing initiatives, it is appropriate to hold detailed, binding term sheet discussions with more than one potential provider.

### On the Elevator

Once your outsourcing team has identified primary and secondary core processes and determined its outsourcing targets, it is time to solicit providers for the process or processes being outsourced. This is one of the most critical components of the outsourcing process, and it must be done properly. To prepare an RFP that will allow you to select the best provider, you must take the following actions:

- Clearly set forth the goals to be achieved by outsourcing, keeping in mind that your primary goal will be to return leadership and management focus to the levels necessary for peak performance. Do not assume that today's level of performance is what is required for the service provider. The goals must fit the organization's needs over the life of the relationship.
- Develop a detailed, realistic timeline for the outsource process. Identify key dates such as RFP release, RFP response, site visits, short list, due diligence, selection, term sheet signing, contract signing, beginning implementation and completing implementation.
- Involve senior management early, often and at key decision points. Be certain senior management understands the scope, goals and timeline. Set realistic expectations. Obtain leadership support.
- Be certain that a wide range of candidates are prequalified before sending the RFP. Consider outsource providers as well as industry players. Perform extensive research to be certain all viable candidates are asked to bid by creating an RFI that clearly defines your needs and evaluating the responses to those needs.

- Clearly define the scope of what is to be outsourced. Once the scope is defined, be sure that the boundaries of what is to be outsourced are clearly established.
- Establish a benchmark based on doing the functions to be outsourced yourself. Understand the cost drivers of self-performing and service levels that will serve as a baseline for the outsourced activity.
- Be certain the RFP provides a clear set of requirements, a clear path forward, and a clear desire for innovation and creativity. Use the RFP to tell people what needs to be done. Do not use the RFP to tell potential providers how to do their jobs. Be certain the full range of requirements is set forth to include slow, typical and high levels of requirements.
- Share the outsourcing process and timeline with each qualified provider. Be sure all candidates are given the same information and opportunity to present their best bid.

Evaluating proposals and choosing your final candidate is a time-consuming process. A key thing to keep telling yourself is "Success is all in the details." You must stay focused and consider all angles when you evaluate proposals, which should be done in three steps.

First, take the proposals and use them to develop a short list. Then, the team should review the proposals to search for viable candidates. There are other actions you can take that complement and supplement the proposal review. These activities include:

- Face-to-face meetings
- Operations site visits
- Post-proposal communications review

The result will be a short list of contenders, and the rigorous evaluation of the finalists to determine who will get the project can begin.

Contrary to popular belief, deciding which of the providers on your shortlist will be your outsourcer involves more than contacting the provider with the lowest

you must evaluate the potential provider's company as a whole and not just its sales team.

Bids are often complex. Be sure all bids address the full scope of the functions to be outsourced. Be sure the evaluation is "apples to apples" and "oranges to oranges." Examine the details of the pricing and do the arithmetic on the pricing proposal for benchmark levels. Do not make assumptions or take the bids at face value.

Contact at least three customers of each potential provider and obtain insights into the provider's performance. Ask a standard set of questions and be certain you obtain provider feedback on everything that gives you concern. If appropriate, go visit customers and view their performance firsthand.

bid and beginning the contract negotiation process. Instead, develop a list of weighted criteria (one that includes cost) and rank each element. The highest performance index indicates the best candidate and, by default, the provider you have selected for your outsourcing initiative. When you have made your decision based on weighted criteria, contact the other providers and let them know that you are not awarding them the contract and, if you feel it would be beneficial, explain why.

Until a binding relationship is established, you should always retain more than one provider. Therefore, do not tell any potential provider they are "the winner" until after a binding term sheet or contract is signed. For larger outsourced contracts, it is appropriate to hold detailed, binding term sheet discussions with more than one potential provider.

# Chapter 8
# STARTING UP THE BOLD OUTSOURCING RELATIONSHIP

"Be prepared to deal with the FUD factor: Fear–Uncertainty–Doubt. People are afraid of the unknown, and it is human nature to resist change."

Outsourcing requires giving up internal control of a business function and trusting others to handle this function for you. It brings together at least two organizations with individual internal structures, terminology, information capabilities and operating philosophies. This chapter delves into the requirements for beginning a successful bold outsourcing relationship—the type that a bold company needs, starting with a discussion of creating the outsource relationship from a leadership perspective as well as a legal one. Then, it describes the process of putting the relationship in motion, including the keys to a successful start-up, how to avoid pitfalls and additional tips.

## Creating an Outsourcing Relationship

The main goal when creating an outsourcing relationship is to effectively evolve what was found in the selection process into a working relationship that takes you through the contracting process to implementation. Throughout this process, you must communicate openly, honestly and without bias. Otherwise, you will be left with false perceptions, unrealistic goals, lowered expectations and a weak relationship that could jeopardize your entire outsourcing initiative.

Therefore, as soon as is practical, you should create a new team—the implementation team—composed of members of both companies to begin the process of creating your relationship. The purpose of the team is to establish multiple touch points between your company and your provider. It should go beyond the provider's sales organization and your outsourcing team and involve the people who are actually going to do the work.

After you have created the implementation team, its first task is to create the outsourcing relationship. This involves:

- Getting the relationship started,
- Determining the relationship structure,
- Selecting a fee structure,
- Validation (relationship due diligence), and
- Setting realistic timeline expectations.

The sections that follow discuss these actions.

*Getting the Relationship Started*

Getting the relationship started involves the following actions:

- **Setting initial expectations:** This process requires full disclosure, open communication and accurate information among all parties. As with any relationship, honesty is the best policy when you discuss expectations. If you are honest with your provider, they are more likely to be honest with you. Treat them as a partner and make them privy to your goals and plans, and work together to set realistic service expectations candidly and openly.

- **Jointly identifying resources up front:** The resources needed to perform the outsourcing functions should be identified in all areas impacting the relationship's success, including financial, operations, legal and technical resources. It is also vitally important to clearly identify the roles and responsibilities of the resources involved in the relationship so that all parties know who will be doing which tasks. The responsibilities must be communicated to both organizations to ensure everyone is aligned.

- **Determining where you are now and your destination:** After you have set initial expectations and identified resources with one another, it is time to tell the provider where you are, then discuss where you want the outsourcing initiative to take both of you. This includes setting goals and milestones and determining how to achieve and measure success. A major area where surprises can destroy relationships is lack of agreement on what is meant by success, so it is important that you take the time to define and determine performance measures.

- **Developing a plan for meeting resistance:** Typically, the internal reaction to outsourcing is to oppose the project, so you must have a plan for easing staff concerns. Be prepared to deal with the FUD factor: Fear-Uncertainty-Doubt. People are afraid of the unknown, and it is human nature to resist change. So, flood people with information. This plan should include explaining to your staff why you are outsourcing and the changes it will bring, sharing your rollout plans, emphasizing the partnering aspect of outsourcing and offering placement plans for the individuals who are not part of your new future or who do not want to be. You might have to take these steps a number of times. Do not be discouraged—eventually, most resistance will recede. See part two of this book for more information on leading and inspiring the people in your organization throughout the outsourcing process.

• **Preparing for employee transition:** An important relationship factor revolves around the transition of employees from the company to the provider. Doing this poorly can kill a relationship. Factors such as compensation, benefits, severance and government regulations must be clearly understood and communicated. Individuals to be transitioned must understand the positive aspects of moving from the periphery of the company to a core group within the provider. Each individual to be transitioned needs to have their personal fears and concerns addressed.

After you have completed these tasks, you are ready to determine your relationship structure.

*Determining a Relationship Structure*

Each provider-client relationship is unique with no absolutes, so structure is important. You are more likely to have a successful relationship with your provider if you both focus on the structure of the relationship. In fact, the Outsourcing Research Council found that outsourcing relationships made the greatest gains when they focused on three areas: structure, management organization and the manager's leadership abilities. With a strong relationship structure, your initiative itself will be strong. To structure your relationship, take these steps:

1. Define jointly what each of you means when you say you want a good relationship.

2. Set the parameters that will help you achieve this good relationship, such as:
    • Metrics and reporting content, calculation and timing
    • A communication plan and resources for both implementation and steady state
    • Problem resolution and development of steering committee
    • Invoicing format and relevant backup data
    • The method or methods you will use to gain consensus, such as written agreement or implicit understanding

3. Address which structure will work best for you and your outsourcing provider based on these parameters by asking some basic questions, such as:
    • What is the size of the outsourcing scope of work?
    • What is the provider's level of experience?
    • Do you want one outsourcing provider to manage everything or do you want to use several providers?
    • What is the geography of the outsourcing initiative? Nationwide? Regional? Global?
    • Are there special requirements involved with the initiative, such as returns,

## Tips for Ensuring a Successful Relationship Structure

Some tips for making sure the structure you have identified is successful are:

- No matter which structure you choose, you must be very clear about accountability and responsibility.
- Communicate, communicate, communicate. The more each of you knows, the better you can work together within your relationship structure.
- Maximize value for both the client and the outsourcing provider. All participants must win within the structure. Make sure that all parties in the structure will benefit from the relationship. A structure that benefits one participant or a group of participants at the expense of others is a poor structure.
- Company cultures can be everything. It is important that each company understands the other's culture and that both can work in harmony so that the relationship structure can evolve. As a result, trust will grow as expectations are met. Open discussions about trust are to be encouraged.

fulfillment, function or customer mandates?
- What tasks will the outsourcing provider expect of us?
- Are we prepared to service the needs of our provider?

4. Discuss the answers to these questions with your provider to gain a better idea of the structure of your relationship.

After you and your provider have determined your relationship structure, the next step is to establish the fee structure for the initiative. Putting a pricing structure in place is an important relationship hurdle.

*Selecting a Fee Structure*

The fee structure for an outsourcing initiative serves as the basis for the service agreement between an outsourcer and a provider. The best fee structures are developed mutually after the parties have explored all the possibilities so that the fee structure allows for the changes inherent in a long-term outsourcing relationship. Fee structures should be as flexible as the relationships that create them. At the highest level the pricing (fee) options are:

- **Fixed cost:** This fee structure works best when the outsourcing initiative involves predictable volumes. In its simplest form, the provider agrees to do the work for a set price rather than being paid on a time and materials basis. A more complex version of this is the service level-driven fixed-price agreement ("fixed-price SLA"). In these cases, the provider must meet predetermined performance levels before they can realize any revenue.
- **Transactional cost:** The transactional-fee structure is the most common pricing model. Basically, a flat fee is charged per unit cost of work.
- **Cost plus:** This pricing option is the actual cost of the initiative plus a percentage fee or flat fee. It is especially effective if your outsourcing project is volatile and is less likely to be applied to a long-term

initiative. This structure is popular with large providers because they make money in every circumstance.

• **Activity-based:** This hybrid fee structure includes a flat fee component and a variable fee component. The variable fee is based on volume and covers those costs that vary for the provider such as labor, maintenance and fuel.

• **Management fee:** The management fee pricing model is structured as a fixed annual charge for required services. Typically, the client is responsible for direct costs as they are billed, and the management fee is used to cover the provider's overhead and profit.

• **Combined structures:** Many fee structures developed between clients and providers are combinations of several structures, such as transaction, cost-plus and management fee.

The best outsourcing fee structure for your company and your provider is likely to be a continuous debate. What is important is that you and your provider explore all the pricing possibilities and their ramifications before you settle on a fee structure. If you both approach setting the fee structure with open minds, a view toward flexibility, full disclosure and no assumptions, you will find the right approach. Then, you can begin discussions about how to build in improvement factors, because most fee structures do not have measures for encouraging continuous improvement, enhanced service or cost reduction. It is important that you and your provider approach this concept at this stage, although it should be done with caution. Then, you will be ready for the next step in the process of creating your relationship: validation, or relationship due diligence.

*Validation (Relationship Due Diligence)*

During validation, clients and providers work together as a team to understand what the other is selling and what is needed. Both must be prepared to change assumptions or make adjustments to their expectations. Your provider should take the RFP and make sure that you clarify it. Your provider should ask probing questions and work toward a more granular level of detail than the RFP provides.

In turn, you should ask your provider for detailed data analysis and ask revealing questions about their proposed solution. During this process, you should also assess your organizations' cultural fit, identifying differing philosophies and determining how to make them work or how to overcome them. Once the validation process is complete, you and the provider can create a timeline.

*Setting Realistic Timeline Expectations*

Before you and your provider get involved in the legal issues necessary for cementing your relationship, you need to develop a realistic and detailed timeline. A list of

## An Example of the Importance of Validation/Due Diligence

Consider this situation. After an exhaustive review of responses to RFIs and RFPs, Company A selected Company X to operate several distribution centers (DCs). Company X had impeccable financials. Its records showed that it was a strong, solvent company with the latest software, and according to its references, its employees were well-trained. Site visits to other DCs managed by Company X revealed efficient operations. So, Company A entered into an agreement with Company X. In the end, however, Company A's outsourcing initiative failed. Why? Because Company A made false assumptions about Company X based on what they read. Company X had the latest software, but unfortunately, its IT staff did not know how to install it on Company A's legacy systems. Company X's operations were efficient because of well-defined processes and methodologies; however, the company did not know how to apply those processes and methodologies in Company A's DC.

This story illustrates one of life's lessons: What looks good on paper doesn't necessarily work well in real life. Company X looked like the perfect candidate to Company A. However, real life

Continues on next page

dates you should determine together include:

1. Due diligence completed
2. Service agreement signing
3. Communication plans:
   a. Internal
   b. Customers and vendors
4. Resource assessment
5. Create project teams
6. Regulatory issues resolution
7. Planning:
   a. Transition
   b. Operations
   c. Technology
8. Benchmarking
9. New equipment/facilities acquisition
10. News releases
11. Go-live dates
12. Training
13. Testing
14. Inventory planning—product movement plans

Discussing these elements and the key dates of the initiative creates common thinking about the process and the next steps. It will also result in the outline of what will become your outsourcing plan. Then, you will be ready to concentrate on forging your legal relationship with your provider.

### The Legal Relationship

To form a strong, mutually beneficial, and successful legal relationship, you need the assistance of experienced legal counsel. Experienced counsel can navigate you through the muddy waters of outsourcing and help you achieve the relationship that will best benefit your company. If you do not have an in-house legal team, we recommend seeking the advice of outside counsel.

It is also critical that you involve counsel *early in the process*. This is because your counsel needs time to understand the drivers behind your decision to outsource and whether the motivation to outsource is to focus on core competency, reduce cost, acquire best of breed technology or processes, free up capital or some or all. To further the relationship building process, your counsel must understand the synergies between you and your provider or providers, how motives are aligned, what the expectations are at the outset and what the success criteria are.

The above requirements dictate early and thorough involvement. Some companies might want counsel present when they identify core competencies to help the legal team gain the understanding of their motivations for outsourcing. Others might bring in the legal team when they are drafting the RFI and searching for recipients of the RFPs. The very latest in the process that you should bring in legal is before you draft the RFP, but it is to your advantage not to wait that long.

Involving the legal team in the RFI improves your selection process dramatically, because your counsel will be familiar with all the players and can contribute to the selection. This also better prepares the legal team when it is time to negotiate.

Your legal team's outsourcing negotiation strategies should include determining whether to negotiate with only one provider or with two. Whether you decide to negotiate with one provider or two, your legal relationship can take several paths during negotiations. Some of the options include binding term sheet to contract, letter of intent or non-binding term sheet to contract, letter of intent to binding term sheet to contract, and contract.

The provider you have selected might try to influence you toward taking the contract path. The problem is the current business climate is so dynamic that companies cannot make forecasts beyond one or two years, and it is rare for anyone to know where their company will be in five years. That is why I recommend leading the negotiations with a binding term sheet, which allows you to settle on the terms of the deal without bogging down the parties in "legalese."

revealed otherwise. What both companies should have done, before signing any agreements, was go through a validation, or due diligence, process. Had they done this, Company A may have realized that it needed to upgrade its legacy systems or Company X might have hired personnel who had experience installing up-to-date software on older systems. Had Company X discussed Company A's DC operations before signing the agreement, they may have realized that the processes needed an overhaul before their workforce took over.

A negotiated term sheet embodies the deal and will be the basis of the agreement. Properly constructed, it makes preparation, negotiation and execution of the definitive agreement a simple process and allows you to continue to evaluate and improve the service provider's proposed changes, technical solutions and legal terms. Ideally, your term sheet should cover everything. For example, it should not differentiate between legal and business issues because nearly all issues are business issues. However, at minimum, the term sheet must integrate commercial, legal, technical and financial issues; balance risk and reward; balance certainty and flexibility; provide price predictability; and plan for exit.

Negotiating an outsourcing term sheet (or agreement or contract) differs from negotiating routine purchase or service agreements, because it usually involves intellectual property, warranties, creative design, epidemic failure, liability and indemnity provisions. So, the contract terms that will be the subject of a great deal of discussion between your company, the legal team and the provider are service levels and performance measures.

Service levels are the mechanisms for enabling the measurement of performance and are often linked to service response times, system performance times and fix times for faults. This part of the agreement must identify each service level clearly and objectively while making sure that those services that are inappropriate for service levels are clearly defined, measurable and achievable as well.

When you and your counsel are negotiating service levels, you should pay particular attention to those service levels that will affect the organization's core functions and its prime business indicators, and how you will determine whether they have been achieved. The failure to achieve service levels can lead to service credits. These are created when the provider does not meet any of the individual performance standards for the service levels set forth in the agreement. In order to be enforceable, these should be a reasonable estimate of the loss that will be suffered as a result of the failure to achieve the service level. You will also want to consider whether these service credits should be an exclusive remedy or whether an aggrieved customer can also make a claim in damages or terminate the agreement.

Performance measures are usually included with service levels, and you and your provider must agree on them prior to signing an agreement. These should be clear, objective Key Performance Indicators (KPI) that are aligned with your strategic direction, are appropriate to the project, and provide readily understood signals of when the provider is succeeding and when improvement is needed. The metrics will vary, depending on the tasks that your provider will perform.

A common practice is to include a provision for benchmarks against which you and your provider periodically compare services and prices with industry best practices. This requires looking outside your organization best-in-class performance comparisons and comparing your business to companies within and outside your industry. Once the metrics are collected, a gap analysis is completed that typically looks at the best-in-class performer within and outside of your industry. This is followed by more analysis to assess the degree to which actual practice changes are necessary to approach or achieve these levels.

Once you and your provider have discussed and established service levels and performance metrics, you can discuss the other parts of your agreement, which should include:

- **Term:** Sets forth the length of the agreement.
- **Schedule:** Describes the key dates for the project.
- **Scope of services:** Spells out exactly what the outsourcer will be doing for your company.
- **Price:** Sets the price of the provider's services and the pricing arrangement.
- **Payment terms:** Describes the method of payment, including the invoice terms, the payment terms, and the terms for addressing changes and evolution over the life of the relationship.
- **Ownership and confidentiality of data:** Clearly states who owns intellectual rights to data and other proprietary information.
- **Governance:** Spells out who has ultimate responsibility over the agreement, who has the authority to make decisions about the initiative, and who addresses issue escalation.
- **Insurance requirements:** Delineates the various types of insurance the outsourcer is expected to provide your company and the amounts of the coverage.
- **Staffing:** Identifies the provider's primary representative as well as their key project, outlines relationships between your company and the provider and describes how to handle subcontractors and other human resource issues.
- **Performance incentives:** Details rewards for exceeding service levels (incentives) or not meeting them (performance bond).
- **Business resilience:** Covers the provider's plans for disaster recovery, business interruption and positive business changes, along with the date for it to be in place, and the terms for periodic review and testing.
- **Representations and warranties:** States past and existing facts, promises that existing or future facts are or will be true, and states that when the term sheet is properly executed, it will be a valid and binding obligation.
- **Warranty of services:** Promises that the provider can and will deliver the services and products on schedule in a diligent manner in accordance with professional standards and the agreement's service levels.
- **Non-solicitation of employees:** States that neither party will try to hire an employee of the other party away from the current employer or convince one to leave his or her employer.

- **Audit:** Sets forth the audit rights for the outsourcing initiative.
- **Liquidated damages:** States what compensation your company will receive from the provider should they fail to meet their obligations and it is determined that this failure was not caused by your company's actions.
- **Indemnification:** Obligates each company to "hold harmless" the other company from losses caused by any willful misconduct or illegal actions on their part.
- **Limitation of liability:** Spells out the outsourcer's liability in terms of your product and its promise to provide services and adhere to the schedule described in the service agreement.
- **Dispute resolution:** Identifies the steps that will be taken to resolve disputes between both companies that have escalated above operational and executive levels.
- **Termination and termination assistance:** Describes how and why each party can terminate the agreement, how the party terminating the agreement will compensate the other, and how termination assistance will be provided should the outsourcer terminate the agreement.
- **Assignability/right to subcontract:** States whether or not the provider can use subcontractors and the procedures to be followed if subcontracting is allowed.
- **Governing law:** Identifies the laws of the states and countries that will govern the agreement and, in particular, any arbitration involved in dispute resolution.
- **Approval or censure:** The legal relationship must define the rights of approval or censure with respect to provider facilities, staff, procedures and so on.

For each portion of the agreement mentioned above, you, your counsel and the provider should make sure everything is clearly stated, that all issues are understood and that the details and schedule for transition steps are included.

The legal relationship must clearly define the details and schedule for transition steps. Key questions that need to be answered include:

- What assets, operations, employees, testing and go-live transition steps need to take place, and who has responsibility and accountability for these to happen?
- What will take place if these do not happen as planned?
- How will you know if these transitions steps occurred or not?

The result of this legal relationship will be a solid foundation for drafting the final contract and executing the service agreement. Then, you can put the outsourcing relationship into motion.

### Putting the Outsource Relationship in Motion: Start-Up

Successful start-ups always have a common underlying theme: effort and contribution from both parties. The real work begins once the contract is signed; the actions leading up to that are just the beginning. Your company cannot afford to be passive during this time. Instead, you must be involved in all aspects of the outsourcing initiative, communicate your needs, and acquire information and input from the outsourcing provider. You should include the provider in planning meetings to discuss strategy and performance. The provider should in turn be responsive to any pertinent changes and communicate any problems or issues encountered as you both move forward. This section shares the keys to a successful start-up, some common pitfalls to avoid during start-up, and some additional tips.

*Keys to a Successful Start-Up*

The keys to a successful start-up are:

- **Selecting the right relationship manager:** Start-up is the time to address the issue of project relationship management and select a relationship manager. This manager must be a team-oriented problem solver, able to address performance issues and results, discuss corrective action and emphasize the need for continuous improvement.
- **Teaming for a strong relationship:** A successful start-up requires you and your provider to create start-up teams. These teams should mirror each other. Therefore, your company and your provider should form teams for the following start-up functions: steering committee, technology (WMS, OM, CMS, and so forth), risk management, product transition, human resources, process documentation and training. These teams work with the relationship manager to control the implementation of the partnership and develop the path for ongoing management of the partnership, so the individuals that make up these teams must be project-focused. Their scope is to support the operators, and they take some of the firefighting, the development and the implementation of processes away from them.
- **Being clear about roles and responsibilities:** Both sides own equal share in contributing to a successful start-up. A major aspect of that is creating and understanding responsibilities and ground rules. This is the time to develop rules of engagement that will facilitate the relationship, such as how often teams should meet, which person has what responsibility during start-up and transition, what are absolute "Nos," and the problem escalation chain. This significantly reduces the chance that you will encounter problems that often occur when there are no ground rules put in place early on.
- **Following a good communication plan:** The first step in developing a communication plan is to set clear expectations up front. Document those communication requirements in the form of a plan, and publish it. An unusual but successful method for making sure that the communication plan is followed is to put the relationship manager at the provider's corporate headquarters. During a recent project, I was struck by the client's simple statement: "You know, it's not the

# Other Relationship Pitfalls

The table below shows some of the other common mistakes companies and outsourcing providers can make during the transition period.

| Providers | Clients |
|---|---|
| Not having executive support | Poor decision-making mechanisms |
| Relying on "boilerplate" information for all pricing | Getting too comfortable with the provider at the expense of others |
| Making last-minute decisions | Not reading/understanding the service agreements and metrics clearly |
| Failing to finalize the term sheet or contract | Making last-minute requests or setting new expectations |
| Not dedicating the integration teams to a sole project | Failing to finalize the contract |
| Missing specific regional Human Resource issues, such as employee quality and quantity | Shortening the lead time or moving up the start date |
| Stopping communication with the client | Maintaining a hands-off attitude, not offering to help |
| Sending implementation team home before the working relationship is in a steady state | Poor or no internal employee communication |
| Not developing start-up/steady state metrics with client | Not accepting any responsibility in the outsourcing relationship |
| Not measuring performance during start-up | Internal team (expertise) not being committed to full implementation |
| Not communicating metrics to employees and translating to individual expectations | Expecting 100 percent from the provider on day one of the contract |
| Letting problems move forward without resolution | Using metrics as a "whip" instead of a tool for managing the relationship |
| Not being proactive with communication, forcing client to initiate | Reacting severely to first quality breakdown |
| Failing to adjust processes and retrain to address problem areas and quality issues | Trying to remove itself as the information source for the project |

TABLE 1. IMPLEMENTATION PITFALLS.

provider's warehouse operation where our relationship manager should be residing. It's the provider's head office." This client truly understood that if they really were going to get this very important relationship started, they had to focus on communication.

- **Go to the site before go-live.** Be familiar with the operation. Be familiar with the people. Be onsite at go-live. Communicate and encourage people. Personally lead the celebration for the success of go-live. Assure the accuracy of data and information at go-live. Be sure the people have the information they need to do their jobs.

*Avoiding Start-Up Pitfalls*

During start-up, you and your chosen outsourcing provider also must be aware of and avoid the following major outsourcing relationship pitfalls:

- **Unrealistic goals:** Setting goals that include going live at full production speed or efficiency with no mistakes is unrealistic and can damage a relationship with the provider. The first 90 (or more) days after start-up are not going to be perfect. Your provider is going to struggle to hit the metric targets during that period as they make the adjustments to work with your company.
- **False perceptions:** In the selection process, the provider's sales team will promise you that everything will run smoothly, and this can lead to false perceptions.
- **Lowered expectations:** Client-provider relationships are labeled as failures when one party does not do what the other expects.

The end results of these pitfalls are non-performance, cost increases and failure to achieve continuous improvement.

An excellent way to prevent these results is to manage expectations early in the relationship, because unrealistic expectations create a shaky foundation for any initiative. One method of managing expectations is to go through the contract and be sure each requirement is being met. Then, review your transition plan, and be sure that each step has been addressed. In other words, work the plan, and do not let time pressures or surprises create a false sense of urgency or even panic. You and your provider should also consider conducting round tables with senior management to address issues and concerns.

*Additional Tips for Putting the Outsource Relationship in Motion*

To be successful during the start-up period, both parties must focus on meeting the following key requirements:

- Have senior management buy-in and commitment.
- Be brutally honest and open, no matter how difficult the news.
- Create a joint sign-off process and have key elements go through that process.
- Celebrate small successes along the way.

- Do not keep the initiative a secret.
- Solve problems as they arise.
- Create a timeline and stick to it.

If you work to make your start-up and early relationship with the provider meet these requirements, work together as a team, have a good communication plan in place and make sure everyone is clear about the rules of engagement, their roles and their responsibilities, the period from provider selection to start-up will be successful. You will be ready to establish your ongoing relationship.

### On the Elevator

Outsourcing is giving up internal control of a business function and trusting others to handle this function for you. Therefore, the relationship between you and your outsourcing provider cannot be taken lightly. Although you may have built a great relationship during the selection process, this is not the outsourcing relationship that will take you through your initiative. Creating the outsourcing relationship involves:

- Getting the relationship started
- Determining the relationship structure
- Selecting a fee structure
- Validation (relationship due diligence)
- Setting realistic timeline expectations

This process is not always going to be perfect, but there are a few things you can keep in mind as you work together to help it along:

It is important that you *involve experienced outsource counsel early.* Your legal team needs time to understand the drivers behind your decision to outsource and what your goals for the outsourcing initiative are. Your legal team's outsourcing negotiation strategies should include understanding your company's negotiating position and objectives in the outsourcing initiative. I recommend leading the negotiations with a binding term sheet that embodies the deal and will be the basis of the agreement. The contract terms that will be the subject of a great deal of discussion between your company, the legal team and the provider are *service levels* and *performance measures*.

An important consideration during this period is who will manage the relationship. The relationship manager should be chosen by both parties. Technical ability is not as important as the ability to lead, make difficult decisions, and manage others. You and your provider should also build teams to foster communication and knowledge transition, and establish rules of engagement to facilitate the relationship. Another aspect of putting the outsourcing relationship in motion that will facilitate the process is the development of a solid communication plan that focuses on the quality of information shared.

Once you have put a continuous improvement process in place, your relationship with your provider has a greater chance of growing, improving, and remaining strong. Most outsourcing initiatives are long term, and if you and your provider communicate well and challenge each other, you will be able to take changes and surprises in stride.

# Chapter 9

# ESTABLISHING THE ONGOING OUTSOURCING RELATIONSHIP

"What makes a happy family? The main thing is the ability to disagree while still trusting each other."

A successful start-up is an indication that an outsourcing initiative is on the right path, but it is a long way from ultimate success. To prevent failure down the road, you must take the relationship you have formed with your outsourcing provider during the period between selection and start-up and build upon it. Investing the time and resources to make the outsourcing relationship work after start-up is necessary if you want the initiative to succeed and flourish.

I have already discussed the early stages of the outsourcing relationship lifecycle—from sending out an RFI to creating the relationship during start-up. In this chapter, I explain the process of building a lasting relationship, the Continuous Improvement process and how to keep the relationship in a steady state. I also offer suggestions for overcoming challenges using inspirational leadership, continual communication, change implementation and future preparedness.

## Building a Lasting Relationship

As you begin the process of building a lasting relationship with your provider, an important thing to remember is there is no "off the shelf" approach to the relationship. Establishing a relationship that is geared toward long-term success is as much an art as it is a science. The first step is to give your outsourcer the same acceptance that you would any new member of your organization. You must recognize that you and your provider will disagree, and that such disagreements are healthy. The trick is communicating properly so the disagreements become an impetus for moving the relationship forward.

Once you have adopted an acceptance mindset and have agreed to communicate openly and honestly with your outsourcing provider, you can build the lasting relationship necessary for outsourcing success. This includes:

- Establishing a regular, ongoing process for business planning, evolution and communication. You and your outsourcing provider must decide the levels and frequency of formal and informal communication and meetings.
- Implementing a rewards structure of gain sharing or goal sharing.
- Making sure there are regular, ongoing executive interactions. Executive communication is critical to the success of your outsourcing relationship.
- Reviewing the RFP and the contract after implementation and identifying surprises, changes and problem areas. The outcome of these discussions will be the identification of opportunities for improvement.
- Measuring performance against the initial goals that were established for outsourcing. This needs to be a full, robust analysis of the implementation and the outsourcing initiative.
- Conducting formal "lessons learned" round table meetings with members of your company alone and between you and your provider.
- Encouraging creativity and innovation on both sides of the relationship. You must be flexible and open to new ideas that will develop along the way.

As with any initiative, a key component of a lasting outsourcing relationship is an emphasis on continuous improvement. Basically, an ongoing process of continuous improvement is required for all outsource relationships to flourish.

### Continuous Improvement and the Outsourcing Relationship

To practice continuous improvement, you and your outsourcing provider need to understand collaboration, cooperation and true partnership. You can accomplish this by making sure you and your provider have:

- **The characteristics of a successful relationship:**
  - Shared vision
  - Shared values
  - Shared expectations
  - Shared commitment
  - Shared confidence in one another
  - Shared responsibility
- **Collaboration:** There must be joint participation and cooperation in the initiative and the relationship, along with confidence and commitment to the success of the initiative. Collaboration, which creates the synergy that drives a successful relationship, must be cultivated. To begin the process of collaboration, you and your provider should foster a collaborative environment by overcoming rigidity, communicating your belief in collaboration, beginning a collaboration revolution and celebrating your success.

- **A plan for long-term success:** You and your outsourcing provider must have a plan for making sure that the gains made during start-up are not lost. To do this, you must look beyond start-up and make sure you have the elements for the initiative to be successful six months, one year, two years and even five years after start-up. During this process, you should consider ways to build on the initiative's long-term success. You must work toward an evolution of the relationship whereby you hold on to the gains made during each initiative milestone and never rest on your laurels. As you continually look for new ways to succeed, you and your provider increase commitment, dedication and cooperation.

- **A true partnership:** In an outsourcing initiative, true partnerships are long-term collaborative relationships between an outsourcer and a provider that are based on trust and a mutual desire to work together for the benefit of the other and the initiative. The goal is to blur identities so that you can focus on the initiative and not on individual companies. Not making distinctions between companies allows you to improve and grow your partnership and ensures outsourcing success. The objective is to create the same synergy between organizations that the collaboration process creates within one organization. This means understanding that the term *relationship* is not synonymous with partnership; instead, a relationship must be transformed into a partnership.

- **The Continuous Improvement Success Path Forward:** The Continuous Improvement Success Path Forward is the methodology for establishing continuous improvement once the collaboration and cooperation between the outsourcer and the provider have been established. The path forward has the following steps:
  1. Establish Continuous Improvement teams.
  2. Conduct outsourcing roundtables regularly throughout the lifetime of the initiative.
  3. Define Continuous Improvement vision and evidence of success.
  4. Define prioritized areas for improvement.
  5. Implement Continuous Improvement team recommendations.
  6. Assess evidence of success.
  7. Define new prioritized opportunities for improvement.

Once you have put a continuous improvement process in place, your relationship with your provider has a greater chance of growing, improving and remaining strong. It will also help create a steady state in your relationship.

# Trouble in Paradise: The Behaviors of a Problematic Outsourcing Relationship

The outsourcing relationship after start-up is not a continuation of the honeymoon. The good communication, understanding and trust that resulted in a successful start-up can be lost without effort. Promises made by sales personnel can come back to haunt you and your provider if they are not addressed. Communication can break down, and the result can be that neither you nor your provider has any idea of what drives the other. In the end, you and your provider may end up looking at one another and saying, "I can't believe we got married" or "This is not the person I married."

You and your provider can prevent this from happening by communicating constantly and learning to recognize the signs that your relationship is in trouble. If you are an outsourcer, the behaviors that can lead to a failed initiative are:

- The elimination of daily relationships between managers of both parties
- The failure to maintain metrics and monitor the relationship
- The failure to accept that although you may have outsourced this operation, the responsibility for your supply

*Continues on next page*

## Steady State for the Outsourcing Relationship

Your outsourcing initiative and the relationship you and your provider create can be bigger than its parts. Just a a family can get more done than just a couple alone, so can you and your provider. What makes a happy family? The main thing is the ability to disagree while still trusting each other and getting along (putting aside personal differences) This means you and your provider must be flexible and be willing to compromise when a problem or unforeseen situation arises.

Another important thing you both should try is to keep the relationship fresh and not get into a rut. In an outsourcing relationship this could mean reviewing the contract and making adjustments. Also, you and your provider should make note of things that worked in one facet of the project and see if they can be applied to other parts in the spirit of continuous improvement. You must also learn to deal with changes—in the project and in the relationship. Most outsourcing initiatives are long term, and if you and your provider communicate well and challenge each other, you will be able to take changes and surprises in stride. The result will be a partnership in a steady state that you can manage.

## Managing the Relationship

Managing your ongoing outsourcing relationship can be compared to taking care of a marriage so that you can get to your silver anniversary celebration. Some of the challenges an outsourcing relationship must overcome in the years that follow implementation include:

- The outsourcer's leadership adds people who are not familiar with the outsourcing initiative or the operation.
- The outsourcing provider's onsite leadership changes without notice or a clear plan.
- Mergers and acquisitions introduce new outsourcing alternatives.
- The outsourcing provider fails to evolve with the business.

- Operations does not focus on continuous improvement.
- Costs keep growing without any plan to contain or reduce the trend.
- One side of the partnership does not invest time, effort and resources into the success of the operation.

The keys to meeting any or all of these challenges and ensuring success in your outsourcing relationship are:

- **Inspirational leadership:** The leadership responsibilities for the months and years after implementation are twofold: maintaining focus on the relationship and understanding that business changes. Therefore, those who manage outsourcing relationships must be collaborative problem solvers who demonstrate their ongoing commitment to the outsource relationship by staying actively involved and investing their time. They must be able to address performance issues and results, discuss corrective action and the need for improvement, rather than telling those involved how to run the business. This is true for the relationship manager and company leaders.
- **Continual communication:** The key to ensuring that changes do not upset the outsource relationship is open and continual communication between you and your outsourcing provider. Regular meetings are the key to fostering open communication. This applies to all levels of the relationship, from company executives to those working in the outsourced function. Continual communication should not stop at the doors of your company. The users of the provider's services should be brought into the process of improving the outsource relationship.
- **Change implementation:** In a long-term relationship, change is inevitable. You and your provider must be prepared to make adjustments to the process. If you have fostered continual communication, it will not be difficult to develop a process with your provider to implement changes as follows:

chain is all yours
- The use of metrics as a whip and not a tool

For the outsourcing provider, the following behaviors lead to trouble:
- Failure to be proactive
- No measurement of performance and reporting
- Failure to develop metrics with the outsourcer
- No explanation of metrics at all

As soon as you, someone in your company or someone in the provider's organization realize that any of the above behaviors are occurring or may occur, you must get together as a team and address them. These problems are not insurmountable obstacles. Return to first principles and ask tough questions. Disregard what was done in the past and address the present and future. You may want to hold more frequent roundtable discussions to work things out.

# Continual Communication: Questions to Ask

Below are some of the questions Tompkins Associates encourages outsourcers to ask as part of a policy of open and regular communication:

- Are we following the contract? If not, is this good or bad?
- Are we following the timelines and responsibilities included in the contract? Is there room for improvement?
- How is the relationship holding up under the changing business climate?
- What changes need to be made to align the outsource relationship with evolving requirements?
- What should we do to keep the relationship fresh and relevant?
- What are our goals for the future of our relationship? How can we make these our provider's goals?
- What can we do to improve communication?
- How can we achieve improvements in performance levels?
- How is the outsourcing relationship affecting customer perception of our company?
- What can we do to stay focused on the correct priorities?

1. Have a documented plan that will provide a point of reference and help prevent surprises. While you develop this plan, you should be sure that your company can implement any changes on its end, as they can be the driving force for success.

2. Take your plan, put it in action and monitor performance, cost and attitude.

3. Document what went right during the process change and what went wrong. You and your provider should discuss both aspects, looking for ways to improve.

4. If you encounter resistance from the outsourcing provider, use the spirit of compromise to bring the reasons for this unwillingness to the surface. If it is based on the process, review it and see if a few adjustments can end the provider's push back. If the other party cites personality differences or is unwilling to compromise after the process review I recommend involving a company with experience in overcoming these challenges.

- **Future preparedness:** It is important that goals for the future of the relationship be established and both the company and the provider accept these goals. Making the future better will not happen unless leadership sets the pace here. All contracts have life spans. You should openly discuss the end of the contract term to let your provider know what you expect. Developing the habit of continually documenting the relationship will prepare you for the end of the contract life and renegotiation. Part of preparing for the future includes considering the possibility that the contract will not be renewed once it has expired. Make sure you have a solid, documented plan for managing the exit and transfer costs. At the end of the contract term there are basically three options: bring the functions back in house ("backsourcing"), extend the contract or take the contract out to bid.

A good outsource relationship will share thinking on these options, and there will be no surprises.

# 'ell-Rounded Outsourcing: Air Products & Chemicals, Inc.

ir Products & Chemicals Inc., Allentown, Pennsylvania, a gases and chemicals company, has been outsourcing
its warehousing operations for more than 20 years. Supervisor Patti Platia works with thirteen 3PLs in North
nerica. Platia has developed a list of attributes she looks for in a third-party logistics provider. These attributes
clude:

The ability to handle all aspects of Air Products' business, including hazmat storage facilities
Regulatory compliance based on commodities stored
Financial stability
Honest and open communications; no "smoke and mirrors"
Very high service levels
A rigorous quality process

Platia asks a lot from the 3PLs, but she is also supportive of them, treating them as integral members of
e Air Products' team. "I work closely between our customer service organization and our warehouses. If issues
nonconformances arise, I investigate the specifics of the situation, see how the provider contributes, and
termine whether our instructions could have led to the situation," Platia says. "Together we decide what we can
to prevent recurrence."

The warehouses and Air Products are in constant contact and work together to head off potential problems.
r example, a 3PL and Air Products are both aware when either party has a new customer service representative
board. They watch carefully to ensure that no problems crop up that a more experienced CSR might catch, and
: their partner know if the new CSR needs additional training.

Air Products finds the right balance in providing oversight. For example, the company provides warehouses
th an operations manual, giving explicit instructions on expected outcomes.

"We let them decide the best way to get to the outcome unless there are areas where we've had problems,
en we give specific instructions," Platia says. "The warehouses have the opportunity to review the manual, and
me to us if they have any questions or would like us to consider a better practice. It's all about working together
meet requirements."

Every year Air Products has a provider challenge program, with each partner competing for recognition as
arehouse of the year. The challenge is scored on a point system, with points accumulated over a year. For
ample, typical nonconformance, such as when a customer calls with a complaint, counts as one point against
e provider. If the provider causes a discharge of a product (from a punctured drum, for example), it is assessed
5 points. Internal issues such as inaccurate billing lose half a point. The top warehouse of the year receives
cognition for its employees.

Maintaining productive long-term relationships with her third-party logistics providers is important to
atia. "Moving to a new warehouse requires a lot of additional time and expense," she says. With a long-term
lationship, "you have a better probability of coming to a mutual resolution" when problems occur. "A lot of the
arehouses have been in our network for 15 years or more. They understand the business, and know what we do,"
atia notes. That knowledge pays off in better service, productivity and quality.'

eslie Hansen Harps, "Logistics Outsourcing: Making a Long-Term Commitment," *Inboundlogistics.com*, July 2002,
ttp://www.inboundlogistics.com/articles/features/0702_feature01.shtml

## Backsourcing: Bringing the Function Back In-House

Part of preparing for the future is being able to respond if there is a clear shift in your business that tells you it's time to be doing an outsourced function yourself. Like outsourcing, backsourcing can be expensive. Bringing a function back in-house should only be done when you have researched the situation and all alternatives, and it becomes clear that backsourcing is the right decision.

If you are not satisfied with some aspect of the outsourcing provider, use the tips in this book to establish or improve an outsourcing relationship before bringing the function back in-house. The expense of backsourcing, especially after the cost of outsourcing in the first place, can be high. Unless there is a significant shift in business that makes both the outsourcing and backsourcing decision good ones, the best way to avoid the resources spent on backsourcing is to never outsource in the first place. But if you do need to backsource, here are seven best practices for going about it.

### Ask, Why Did We Outsource?

The first best practice of backsourcing is to understand why the functions were outsourced in the first place so the decision to backsource can be appropriately evaluated. Various reasons for outsourcing can be found in chapter six of this book. Once these reasons to outsource are understood, then it is time to evaluate how outsourcing did or did not meet your objectives. The obvious choices to be made at this point are to continue to use the same provider, have a new beginning with the same provider, move to a new provider or backsource the function. Do a full review of these reasons, and only when a clear justification of backsourcing is made should you act.

### Consider All Legal Issues

A key consideration when making the backsource decision is what the contract says about removing the outsourced business from the provider. Is the term of the relationship complete? If it is, what notification period is required to remove the outsourced business from the provider? Have you met the notification requirements?

If the term of the contract is not complete, are there early termination penalties? Does the contract have a built-in exit strategy? Does the contract define a transition period, process and strategy? What are the duties and responsibilities of the provider? Is there contract guidance on confidential information, product protection and insurance during transition? If terminating early, are there dispute resolution requirements that need to be addressed? It is quite clear that just as one must have early and significant support from counsel during outsourcing, so too is this support required during backsourcing.

*Gain Clear Commitment*

The decision to backsource should be made with the understanding that your organization has committed to reinvest in this portion of your business. If this commitment is not clear, the backsourcing decision needs to be re-evaluated. If lack of commitment by upper management was part of the reason for outsourcing, then ask what has changed that would now make backsourcing this operation a success.

Lack of commitment to provide the leadership, staff, equipment, facilities, systems and capital to perform the outsourced function inside will doom the backsourcing to failure. There needs to be a careful and well-thought-out assessment of all resources required to successfully backsource. And remember that these resources may no longer exist since the outsourcing was implemented and may need to be obtained anew. There must also be adequate management assigned to oversee the backsourcing as well as to manage the functions once returned.

*Figure Out What Has Changed*

Chances are very good that the systems, functions and processes you outsourced are considerably different than the functions and processes you backsource. Like all businesses, your organization continues to evolve, and it would be highly unusual if your outsource requirements have not evolved as well. Therefore, one of the most challenging hurdles to clear involves fully investigating and understanding if the knowledge base you had of the outsourced function is still the knowledge base needed to backsource the function today. This requires a full review, documentation of the current requirements and documenting the process design.

*Plan, Plan, Plan!*

The amount of planning required for successful backsourcing does not vary considerably from the amount of planning required for successful outsourcing. The process as it should be applied to backsourcing involves the following steps:

- Define your backsourcing team.
- Define the backsourcing requirements.
- Develop the backsourcing business plan and backsourcing schedule.
- Assess skills and readiness to successfully backsource.
- Establish a cooperative relationship with the current provider and define communication protocols.
- Clarify roles and responsibilities and the legal relationship with the outsource provider.
- Begin the phased approach of bringing the business back in-house.

• Maintain a relationship with the outsourced provider of teamwork, open communications, cooperation and collaboration.
• Close out the relationship by handling all loose ends and details.

*Communicate, Then Communicate More*

Notify the outsource provider of your decision to backsource as early as possible and communicate in a way that begets a culture of cooperation. This timeframe may be considerable, and requirements of the business may need to be defined up to 18 months prior to the actual conversion. At the appropriate time, communicate to all constituents the goals, objectives, schedules and plans of the backsourcing initiative. Do not naively believe that people will understand what is happening. Open, honest and timely information is required by all to facilitate a smooth transitioning of the outsourced functions back in-house. As George Bernard Shaw wrote, "The problem with communication is the illusion that it has occurred." Be certain that your communication hits home.

*Focus Contingency Planning on the Customer*

Never, ever, ever forget about the impact backsourcing can have on the customer. Develop a contingency plan to cover as broad a set of business continuity issues as is realistic. The contingency plan must fully address customer needs and make the ongoing satisfaction of the customer a key objective. Ensure that the customer is fully briefed on the backsourcing initiative and participates in the development of contingency plans.

### Signs of a Successful Initiative

You and your provider are likely to have a successful initiative if you follow the plans and processes discussed in this chapter from the time of selection to the end of the contract. You can tell you have a successful initiative by looking for five simple signs:

• All expectations are exceeded.
• All performance measures are made and the bar is raised.
• The outsourcing provider is invisible; in other words, the provider "looks like the client."
• The end of the term is simply a renewal process.
• Every success is celebrated in a fun environment.

If you and your provider see these signs, then it is likely you both will be celebrating every success.

## n the Elevator

Managing an outsourcing relationship is not easy. There are numerous challenges o overcome. The keys to meeting these challenges and ensuring success in your outourcing relationship are leadership, continual communication, implementing change nd preparing for the future. If the business climate changes, it might be necessary to acksource, or bring the outsourced function back into your organization. This can be xpensive.

As you then begin the process of building a lasting relationship with your provider, n important thing to remember is there is no "off the shelf" approach to the relationhip. Establishing a relationship that is geared toward long-term success is as much n art as it is a science. To create the right kind of partnership with your outsourcing rovider, you and your provider must function as a cohesive, collective whole.

You and your provider are likely to have a successful initiative if you follow the plans nd processes discussed in this chapter from the time of selection to the end of the conact. You can tell that you have a successful initiative by looking for five simple signs:

- All expectations are exceeded.
- All performance measures are made and the bar is raised.
- The outsourcing provider is invisible; in other words, the provider
  "looks like the client."
- The end of the term is simply a renewal process.
- Every success is celebrated in a fun environment.

# Part 3

**Business Resiliency
and the
Bold Organization**

# Chapter 10

# THE CASE FOR BUSINESS RESILIENCE: VULNERABILITY AND DISRUPTION

"Complex, global supply chains open all the companies in the chain to greater vulnerability, often in ways that are not immediately obvious."

Consider the following events:
- A terrorist attack
- A Category 4 hurricane
- The outbreak of a disease that affects livestock or crops
- A cooling system failure in a server room
- Oprah endorses a product on her show

What do they have in common? They can all affect a company's normal business patterns, causing a disruption in business. Although most people think that a disruption means something that interrupts business operations, this is not necessarily so. A disruption can also be a surge in business to meet new, unexpected demand or a new pricing strategy by a competitor that kills demand for your product. Both surges and drops in demand can bring about a fundamental change to business—changes that interrupt or alter business as usual.

Business disruptions can do immeasurable harm to a company. They can keep companies from delivering on promised goods and services to their customers, and they can create a domino effect throughout a supply chain. The impact of these disruptions can be drastic, and not just in terms of business loss or serious reductions in revenue. There is also the fact that they reveal, sometimes internally and sometimes publicly, the vulnerability of business and how much of our supply chains can be out of our control.

The good news is that business vulnerability and disruption need not destroy your company or hack holes into your supply chain that take years to fix. Businesses can mitigate vulnerability or even use the adversity that comes with it to soar past their competitors. The secret to doing either of these is business resiliency—the ability to bounce back after a business disruption.

In this part of this book, I tackle the topic of business resiliency. This chapter focuses on business vulnerability and why it is critical. Chapter 11 discusses bold business resiliency. The Appendix offers a series of assessments for helping you determine your level of business resiliency.

## Vulnerability

Companies have always had to consider what might happen if something caused them to lose connections with suppliers or if great quantities of products were destroyed in a disaster. The idea of planning for a loss of business or product isn't new. Ford went to great extremes in its early days to try to make sure they had everything they needed on hand at all times to build their cars. They bought glass manufacturing plants, tire manufacturing plants and other companies so they would always have what they needed on hand. Later in the 20th century, many companies thought that carrying a lot of inventory was the secret.

The problem with extreme verticalization like Ford's is that it does not allow a company to excel at every function and can even prevent the company from excelling at anything. In the case of stockpiling finished goods, the costs can far outweigh having a part or product on hand when it is needed. As we have witnessed over the past few decades, companies, for the most part, have deverticalized. As you read in the outsourcing section of this book, the push in business is to divest a company of those functions not identified as primary core or secondary core. The result is an increase in outsourcing. Meanwhile, those companies still in the business of manufacturing are practicing just-in-time and lean manufacturing. The result is that companies have to rely much more heavily on their supply chains to help them get their products to customers. This reliance has created much more complex global logistics networks and supply chains.

At the same time, the demand for reducing time to market has put added pressure on these complex chains to move materials, parts and WIP around the globe quickly. Companies want to minimize inventory of finished goods so they can be more nimble. They want to synchronize supply to demand. But when you move offshore, you increase lead time, and this makes it more challenging to be nimble.[28] These factors—the complex, global supply chains, the need for speed and to be lean in every aspect of business—have made companies much more vulnerable to a serious business interruption that can affect profitability. There are two types of vulnerability here: the vulnerability caused by the new breed of supply chain and the vulnerability caused by huge reductions in inventory. Let's take a look at each.

---

[28] "In Depth: Global Supply Chain—Mastering the Complexity Challenge in the Global Supply Chain," *Supply & Demand Chain Executive*, August/September 2005, http://www.sdcexec.com/article_arch .asp?article_id=5983

*oday's Supply Chains*

For several years now, we've heard about the complex supply chains that Fortune 00 companies like Wal-Mart, GM, Nike and Dell have created. These companies have acilities, outsourcing providers and suppliers located all over the world. Parts manufac-ired in Asia with copper from Chile can be added to parts made in Canada that are then hipped to the U.S. for final assembly and distribution.

Consider Eaton Corporation, a manufacturer of fluid power and electrical components. Until 2004, the company was content to take a localized approach to logistics, even though ie company has steadily become more global by opening manufacturing plants all over the world. In 2004, they decided to outsource their logistics functions. However, in the end, in-tead of having one logistics provider, they opted to use three providers from three different arts of the globe (the U.S., Asia and Europe). They plan to find another logistics provider in Latin America.[29] This is good outsourcing, but it is clearly also an increase in complexity.

The days of supply chains being in only one or two locations are gone. Also gone re the days when only one region was a source for materials, another one for manufac-iring, and another one for assembly. Companies are now sourcing products overseas n new ways—they are not simply picking the lowest cost location as sources for their oods. They have decided to manufacture and use goods in several locations worldwide o they are not dependent on only one source.

For example, Peachtree Fabrics, an Atlanta-based company, has moved a significant mount of its manufacturing to China, Italy, Belgium, Korea, Turkey and India. The company mports its fabric into the United States mainly from China and Italy. In China, the fabrics re shipped from the port of Tianjin to the port of Long Beach, California. From Long Beach, hey are transported by rail to Atlanta, where they go through customs. After that, they're ransported by truck to Peachtree's distribution center. From Italy, the fabrics are consolidated rom different vendors in a facility in Milan and either shipped in containers to the port of Charleston and then trucked to Atlanta, or flown from Italy to Atlanta, where the fabrics clear ustoms before ending up at the Peachtree DC.[30] Efficient, yes, but significantly more complex.

Trying to describe one of today's supply chains is almost as difficult as staying on op of it. The parts that go into manufacturing almost anything today are mind boggling. n his book, *The Resilient Enterprise*, Yossi Sheffi, a professor at MIT, describes just one f the parts involved in manufacturing a GM car, including the raw material sources and he various places where pieces of that car are put together.[31] I tried a similar exercise

---

Roger Morton, "Measuring a Supply Chain from End to End," *Logistics Today*, June 2006, http://www.logisticstoday.com/displayStory.asp?nID=7950

"Mastering the Complexity Challenge," http://www.sdcexec.com/article_arch.asp?article_id=5983

Yossi Sheffi, *The Resilient Enterprise: Overcoming Vulnerability for Competitive Advantage.* (Cambridge, MA: MIT Press, 2005).

with a Whirlpool washing machine. It has a motor, a transmission, a pump, two tubs, a balance ring, bearings, a drive, agitator, hinges, hoses, controls and switches, all manufactured literally around the world. These parts are made of different raw materials that are once again outsourced from many different countries. The machine is put together with bolts, by welding and with glue. Whirlpool operates manufacturing plants in 13 countries and has a massive distribution network. Just when I thought I had a handle on their supply chain, in March 2006, Whirlpool bought Maytag, inheriting its suppliers and logistics networks. A complex supply chain has just doubled in complexity.

With so many links spread far and wide, you can see why these supply chains make companies vulnerable. Multi-sourcing provides some security, but also involves more people and more systems, which open a company to a greater likelihood that something could occur to stop the flow of goods and products through their supply chains. The fact that more and more companies are part of these chains also means that transportation is becoming a prime commodity, as ports experience double-digit growth, the demand for rail capacity increases and trucking companies close their doors because of a driver shortage. The demand is beginning to outstrip the availability of efficient transportation, and without it, the trading world can come to a virtual standstill, as demonstrated by the west coast port lockout of 2002. The distance between links, the different regions involved, the different time zones involved and the different languages spoken in the regions all heighten a business's vulnerability to disruption.

To put this in perspective, supply chain disruptions create three main types of vulnerabilities: supply, operations and demand. Supply vulnerabilities prevent raw material or parts getting to the assembly line. Operations vulnerabilities keep any business in the supply chain from operating normally. Demand vulnerabilities keep the finished product from getting to the customer.

Basically, we have exposed ourselves to so much more with these new supply chains. If you take the five events I listed at the beginning of this chapter and apply them to a supply chain, the consequences are as mind-boggling as the supply chains themselves. Here are some examples:

- A terrorist attack that grounds flights would disrupt Peachtree, because it flies fabrics from Italy to Atlanta.
- A Category 4 hurricane that shuts down oil refineries would disrupt the flow of the petroleum Whirlpool needs to make its washing machines.
- A suspected livestock disease that closes the borders of a European country to pre vent possible contamination in neighboring countries can make trucking of goods difficult for Eaton.
- A cooling system failure in a server room will eventually shut down servers because most are designed to stop running if the temperature in their environments

reaches a certain level. This could halt the flow or storage of critical information that any of these companies need to communicate and collaborate with their supply chain partners.

• A televised profile of Oprah that takes us on a tour of her home, where she shows off her latest Whirlpool washer and dryer duo, could significantly increase the demand for that duo—demand that is greater than current manufacturing levels.

These examples are just the tip of the iceberg. There are other consequences associated with these events that might not be felt immediately but could be devastating. There is the famous example used to demonstrate the chaos theory: A butterfly in Brazil flaps its wings, which sets off a chain of environmental events that ends with tornadoes in Texas. To use one more example from our list, the oil refineries closed by the Category 4 hurricane might reopen after a week or two and be back in production. However, if the trucking companies that transport the oil in tankers across the U.S. are still closed because they lost most of their drivers to evacuations and injury, that oil isn't going anywhere. This is a very simple example, but I've used it to make an important point. Complex, global supply chains open all the companies in the chain to greater vulnerability, often in ways that are not immediately obvious.

*Little or No Inventory*

Customers today are savvy and loyal, but they are also very demanding. When they want something, they want it right away. They also want the product exactly as they imagine it and are not happy if they're told to take a green sofa rather than a blue one because that is what is currently in stock. Dell and other companies have helped create a new generation of customers—this generation expects their products to be made based on their specifications. The days of "We will build it, and they will come" are gone. Instead, companies are focusing on "getting the right product to the right customer right when they need it" and "getting customers exactly what they want exactly when they want it." The reality today is truly that one size fits one.

This seems to be contradictory to the idea of lean manufacturing and just-in-time manufacturing, both of which stress carrying as little inventory as possible. Actually, the two go hand in hand. The secret is synchronizing supply and demand with production and logistics partners so that the parts needed for the final product that the customer has designed can be delivered quickly. This system was first introduced to the world by Toyota, which has become famous for its production system. The basic tenets of the system are echoed in the production system of other automakers, as well as other durable goods and chemical companies.

The theory of postponement is another method that companies are using to reduce inventory. This theory involves postponing the final stages of manufacturing so products

## The Cost of a Disaster

Ricky M. Magalhaes, a security specialist who has worked as a consultant and IT technical specialist, recently put together a list of the possible costs to a company if a disaster disrupts business.

- Revenue loss
- Brand image loss and recovery
- Loss of share value
- Loss of interest on overnight balances; cost of interest on lost cash flow
- Delays in customer accounting, accounts receivable and billing/invoicing
- Loss of control over debtors
- Loss of credit control and increased bad debt
- Loss of revenue for service contracts from failure to provide service or meet service levels
- Lost ability to respond to contract opportunities
- Penalties from failure to produce annual accounts or produce timely tax payments
- Where company share value underpins loan facilities, share prices could drop and loans be called in or be re-rated at higher interest levels
- Cost of replacement of buildings and plant
- Cost of replacing equipment
- Cost of replacing software
- Replacing staff that may have been lost because of disaster
- Salaries paid to staff unable to undertake billable work
- Salaries paid to staff to recover

Continues on next page

can be finished in accordance with the customer's demands. Basically, companies store generic product in the warehouse until they receive a customer order. At this point, the warehouse transforms the generic product into a finished product to meet the customer's order. This has numerous benefits, including increased levels of customer satisfaction, because back orders are reduced, responsiveness is increased and customization is enhanced. Also, manufacturing can plan, schedule, consolidate and balance production runs at the most economical lot size rather than on a SKU by SKU basis. The bottom line is that companies that use the theory of postponement increase inventory turns, reduce SKU reconfiguration and reduce levels of obsolete and slow inventory.

Unfortunately, while such practices realize significant cost benefits for the producers, they also open up a company's vulnerability. As with the complex supply chains, because these practices require a dependence on external companies, the possibility of a business disruption is greater. A clothing company's distribution center in Oshkosh, Wisconsin might be fine, but if the Asian tsunami of 2004 prevents the company from getting buttons and blue jeans because the factories where they're made are destroyed, or the workers are scattered or missing, then the company is not going to be able to receive or ship out clothing on schedule.

The synchronization involved in carrying as little inventory as possible also requires almost flawless communication and software. A great deal of automation and integration goes into this aspect of inventory management. There are supply chain planning and execution systems, telecommunication systems, gate entry management systems at the ports, web-based collaboration systems, tracking systems, GPS, RFID and even differential GPS. There is email, phone, wireless and wire communication. What do you think a failure of a crucial server or the loss of a satellite network would do to this tenuous synchronization network? Or suppose the people who are needed to input data, or attend a collaborative teleconference, or load goods on a truck were not there. In all of these circumstances, there is likely to be a business disruption—and these are the other reasons that little or no inventory and the need for speed make companies vulnerable to disruptions. The next section is an overview of a business disruption and its stages.

## Anatomy of a Disruption

Although there are different types of disruptions, ranging from short and minor to huge and devastating, their composition is basically the same. A disruption has these stages:

1. **Event:** This is the cause of the disruption, which is likely to be a disaster, an accident, an intentional act (like a strike), a materials shortage or a sudden, unpredicted spike in demand.

2. **Impact:** This is the adverse effect that the event has on business, such as loss of materials, damaged facilities, reduced staff, halted production or perishing goods.

3. **Initial reaction:** This includes the actions taken to immediately mitigate or stop the adverse effects of the event, such as first response, stopping machinery or servers, opening negotiations or sourcing needed materials from somewhere else.

4. **Delayed reaction:** This includes the actions taken when the business is impacted adversely over time, usually in ways not originally foreseen when the event occurred. Consider examples such as finding workarounds for closed airports and borders after a terrorist attack, no transportation networks after a disaster, re-locating to a temporary facility or loss of productivity over time because workers are striking.

5. **Recovery:** These are the actions taken after the full impact is realized and usually include restarting production, making repairs, overtime, opening

---

work backlog and maintain deadlines
- Cost of re-creation and recovery of lost data
- Loss of cash flow
- Interest value on deferred billings
- Penalty clauses invoked for late delivery and failure to meet service levels
- Loss of customers (lifetime value of each) and market share
- Loss of profits
- Additional cost of credit through reduced credit rating
- Recruitment costs for new staff on staff turnover
- Training/retraining costs for staff
- Fines and penalties for non-compliance
- Liability claims
- Additional cost of advertising, PR and marketing to reassure customers and prospects to retain market share
- Additional cost of working, administrative costs, travel and subsistence
- Potential prosecution for non-compliance and contract adherence

Other aspects of business like communication, buildings, office equipment, stationary, water supplies, electrical supplies and others add even more costs.[5]

---

[5] Ricky M. Magalhaes, "Security Series: Disaster Recovery Tactics that Ensure Business Continuity," WindowSecurity.com, 11 Jan. 2005, http://www.windowsecurity.com/articles/Disaster-Recovery-Tactics-Part1.html

temporary facilities, or, in the case of a spike in demand, ramping up production. Often, recovery is not simple or quick. We have seen this in the effects of Hurricane Katrina on the Gulf Coast. As I write this, it is almost the one year anniversary of Hurricane Katrina, and the world is still feeling the effects of shifted inventories, driver shortages, closed roads and badly damaged communication systems.

These stages are all related to one another. How a company handles the stages after the first stage can determine the time required to recover.

A stage that is often not given enough attention is the delayed reaction stage. This is because often a business is so busy trying to react to immediate trauma or distress that no thought is given to what the long-term effects might be. A good example is a severe headache. When you have a severe headache, you see immediate relief with a pain reliever. That takes care of the pain then and there and gets you back to work. But what if that severe headache means something else? What if it's an indication that you're getting the flu, or worse, that you might be having a stroke? Pain relievers are an instant reaction to your headache, but they might not be the long-term solution.

Another important thing to remember is that recovery may not mean a return to normal. The business disruption might have been severe or unexpected enough that the company was greatly damaged or has lost its role in key supply chains. On the other hand, in some cases, the recovery stage reaps great rewards for a company, and its business increases or goes off in a better, more profitable direction. As I stated earlier in the chapter, a company does not have to be ruined by any or all of these stages. Many companies bounce back in less time than you might think after a business disruption or unusually high demand for a product. It is their level of business resilience that allows them to do this, and that is why business resilience is critical to success in today's marketplace.

## Making the Case for Business Resiliency

When you combine the changes in the supply chain with the series of disasters that have happened since the beginning of the 21st century (9/11, the Asian tsunami of 2004, Hurricane Katrina, the earthquakes in Turkey, bombings in Spain and London), you can see why business resiliency has become more than just a phrase. Business resiliency is on everyone's minds these days—and for good reason. If your business is not prepared with a plan for how to handle a temporary knot in your supply chain or how to survive a disaster, then your business will suffer and may not survive.

The problem that companies face is that the concept of business resiliency is still new. Except for those companies that have learned to expect continuous business disruptions, many companies are still struggling with the concept. There is a tendency to look or the cause of the disruption and tackling survival that way, which can be helpful. But is not as important as other activities—such as researching the planning and recovery at companies with frequently disrupted supply chains have in place, or determining ow to add redundancy to operations without driving up costs. Another critical component of resilience is collaboration, both inside and outside the organization—all along e supply chain. All of this can be boiled down into five steps:

1. **Assess:** It's important that you understand where your company is in terms of preparation for disruption. This means reviewing your current supply chain, your forecasting and planning abilities, and communication in detail. Your focus should be identifying gaps and bottlenecks, identifying the areas that are critical to supply chain performance and identifying vulnerability.

2. **Plan:** Look for trouble. Know your industry, current trends and cost structures, and think about what could go wrong. Then, make sure that your supply chain performance and business processes are adjusted accordingly. This means performing diagnostics and making improvements. Make sure your supply chain is flexible to withstand disruptions.

3. **Communicate:** Business resiliency is not possible without a responsive supply chain. You are not in this alone—so, as you plan, detail and assess your supply chain, communicate openly and honestly with your supply chain partners, stakeholders and customers. They need to understand the changes you are planning to make, the objectives you have identified and what you expect from them.

4. **Evaluate.** Watch your supply chain. Use tangible, realistic performance measures to determine how your company and your supply chain are doing. Don't forget to document any actions and consequences involved.

5. **Re-evaluate.** This is critical. Nothing should be set in stone, because that is the opposite of resiliency. Supply chains are fluid entities, and so is business, so you need to review and rank your operations periodically, as well as update your plans. You should identify changes and considerations that were not apparent during your original assessment. This is a good time to rely on your customers—ask them how you're doing and ask them to tell you how you could improve. Do this regularly.

Following these steps is not easy. Detailing your supply chain can take time, because odds are that it crosses a number of borders and time zones. Researching your industry and trends while trying to stay on top of all the things that can affect your operations means spending a lot of time reading and asking questions. Communicating with partners, stakeholders and customers can also be tricky—cultures, time zones and languages are all factors in this, along with the inherent tendency for companies to protect information. Evaluating and re-evaluating also requires a commitment from

## Plan: Limited Brands

A port lockout in the U.S. west coast due to a labor dispute should have had Limited Brands on the ropes. Limited Brands is the parent company of Victoria's Secret, Bath & Body Works, Express, Limited Stores and Henri Bendel. The company imports thousands of containers annually from factories around the world, relying heavily on the west coast ports. In 2004, 75 percent of its containers traveled through Southern California ports. Instead of waiting days and months for merchandise to arrive at its Columbus, Ohio DCs, the merchandise was delayed only about two days. The company also found trucks to carry its goods and was successfully able to maintain service levels.

How did they manage this? Paul Marshall, director of inbound logistics for Limited Brands, says they saw it coming. According to Marshall, the company began to notice a deterioration of the level of service on the west coast, and they decided it was a trend rather than an abnormality. To prevent taking a big hit to their business, the company got together and came up with an action plan. The plan included:

- Keeping everyone informed. At the first sign of trouble, the company alerted their customers so they could adjust performance expectations and plan their inventory. Limited Brands also gathered

*Continues on next page*

everyone involved to be open to change and suggestions for improvement. You also have to have customers who are willing to provide honest feedback.

Don't let this discourage you. If your company is populated with inspirational leaders, has embraced the robust outsourcing strategy outlined in the previous part of this book, and has an innovative plan for business resiliency, then you can overcome any business disruption or even use them to your advantage. In the Appendix, I show you how to get started on the five steps to business resiliency by sharing some of the supply chain assessments Tompkins Associates has used to help organizations determine their resiliency levels.

### On the Elevator

Business disruptions can do immeasurable harm to a company. They can keep companies from delivering on promised goods and services to their customers, and they can create a domino effect throughout a supply chain. The impact of these disruptions can be drastic, not just in terms of business loss or serious reductions in revenue, but also in the fact that they reveal, sometimes internally and sometimes publicly, the vulnerability of business and how much of our supply chains can be out of our control. The good news is that business vulnerability and disruption need not destroy your company or hack holes into your supply chain that take years to fix. Businesses can mitigate vulnerability or even use the adversity that comes with business disruption to soar past their competitors. The secret to doing either of these is business resiliency—the ability to bounce back after a disruption.

Today's companies are much more vulnerable to a serious business interruption that can affect profitability. There are two types of vulnerability: the vulnerability caused by the new breed of supply chain, and the vulnerability caused by huge reductions in inventory. Complex, global supply chains open all the companies in the chain to greater vulnerability, often in ways that are not immediately obvious. The synchronization involved in carrying as little inventory s possible requires dependence on external companies and almost flawless communication and software, both of which make a company more vulnerable to disruptions.

A disruption has these stages:

1. Event
2. Impact
3. Initial reaction
4. Delayed reaction
5. Recovery

These stages are all related to one another. How a company handles the stages after the first stage can determine the time required to recover. The problem that companies face is that the concept of business resiliency is still new and, except for those companies that have learned to expect continuous business disruptions, many companies are still struggling with the concept. There is a tendency to look for the cause of the disruption and trying to survive that way. This can be helpful, but it is not as important as other activities, which can be boiled down to:

1. Assess
2. Plan
3. Communicate
4. Evaluate
5. Re-evaluate

If your company is populated with inspirational leaders, has embraced the robust outsourcing strategy outlined in the previous part of this book, and has an innovative plan for business resiliency, then you can overcome any business disruption or even use them to your advantage.

information about their supply chain partners and industry conditions. They also communicated with carriers weekly by conference call to coordinate and prioritize incoming shipments.

- Remaining agile. The company shifted its shipping patterns, using the ports of Seattle and Tacoma, along with keeping a smaller presence in Southern California.
- Consolidating when possible. The company decided to single source their consolidation to improve flexibility and communication.
- Keeping options open and using different modes of transportation. Limited Brands worked with different carriers that offered services to more than one port and also had strong intermodal shipping relationships. They looked for providers that could switch between intermodal and trucking easily.[1]

---

[1] Paul Marshall, "It's All in the Planning," *DC Velocity*, October 2005, pp. 28–29.

# Chapter 11
# THE BUSINESS RESILIENCY PLAN

"In these days of lean supply chains and globalization that create greater distances between facilities and supply chain partners while making next-door neighbors of us all, you cannot be resilient without a plan."

As you learned in Chapter 10, resilience is important now more than ever. The pace of business has accelerated, and the velocity of events is greater. This makes us more susceptible to disruptions, unexpected surges and declines in demand. As you have more things occurring, the likelihood of something unexpected happening is greater. Therefore, to prepare for business interruption and vulnerability, you need a business resiliency plan that can protect and improve your customer satisfaction, brand reputation, people and profits while providing a proactive, comprehensive and robust strategy for achieving and maintaining competitive advantage. It must create a flexible and adaptive underlying operational infrastructure that also protects against the unknown, unexpected threats or challenges. This plan should encompass not only your internal operations, but your external networks and your supply chain as well.

After you have the plan in place, you must communicate it, evaluate it and reevaluate it to keep it fresh and to make adjustments as the world around us continues to change. Remember, the day before 9/11, we couldn't have known that two planes could take down two major skyscrapers that housed numerous companies doing business all over the world; but now we do. On August 26, 2005, we had only imagined what a Category 4 hurricane might do if it hit a major business center or port, but now we know how people and businesses were affected.

In this chapter, I discuss how to create and implement a business resilience plan that is a critical part of how you do business, including what you should do before you start developing the plan and what elements are necessary for a successful plan. I then show you the importance of communication to the plan and to business resiliency as a whole, and the evaluation and reevaluation process.

## Getting Started: Preparing for the Plan

The process of developing a business resilience plan starts with the creation of a business resiliency planning team. The makeup of this team is critical and should include members from all functional areas in the company, because business vulnerability and resiliency affects everyone. The members of the team should be inspirational leaders with a good understanding of the processes in their functional areas and how those processes would be affected by both interruptions and surges in demand. Inspirational leaders will contribute intelligently and knowledgeably to the process of developing your business resiliency plan. They can react to issues quickly and decisively, putting forth solutions while communicating with everyone involved, especially those high up in the organization.

The business resiliency planning team should also include members from outside the physical boundaries of your company, such as representatives from your suppliers and outsourcing providers. Including them is a bold move. You might meet with some initial internal and external resistance. Be firm when you encounter it. Bold, resilient organizations rely heavily on outsourcing providers and supply chain partners to help them achieve the flexibility, adaptability and redundancy they need to be bold. Take your inspirational leadership skills and use them to persuade key players from outside your company to join the team. The results will probably surprise and please them, and everyone will win when an unexpected situation occurs.

After you have created your team, you should choose a representative to be the single point of contact between the team, the rest of your company, your supply chain partners, outsourcing providers and the executives of your company. Then, the team should gather the results of your assessments, which should be:

- A list and analysis of all significant threats, vulnerabilities and dependencies related to critical business processes throughout your organization and your supply chain at both functional and geographic levels.
- An evaluation of your existing disaster recovery, business continuity and crisis management plans (if you have one or more of them).
- Metrics that show the business impacts of gaps, vulnerabilities and risks on critical business process and operational infrastructures.

This information is critical for the formulation of your business resilience plan.

## Goals and Strategies for a Business Resiliency Plan

A business resiliency plan should have goals for ensuring that a company is flexible, adaptable, redundant and secure, because these characteristics can not only ensure resiliency but can also help a company overcome disruptions, surges and broken supply chain links. In *The Resilient Enterprise*, Yossi Sheffi describes steps for reducing vulnerability that also make excellent goals:

- **Reducing the possibility of disruptions:** This includes taking the information compiled from your assessment (described in the Appendix) and using it to focus on how to detect and identify a disruption quickly and correctly. Statistical process control tools are useful for meeting this goal. You also will want to consider measures that are not "one-size-fits-all" but feature different layers of defense against disruptions, surges and disasters.

- **Learning and sharing for safety and security:** Thanks to the Internet, information and organizations that deal with the very real problems of safety and security are readily available. You can access safety and security standards from many organizations, and many welcome new members to maintain a continuing dialog about keeping your assets, company, employees and supply chains safe and secure. This information and these organizations, along with internal collaboration with your employees and compliance with regulatory bodies, can help you meet this goal.

- **Building in redundancies:** This goal, when applied to production, is like walking a tight rope. If you build in too much redundancy using multiple suppliers, safety stock, extra capacity, added workers and low utilization you run the risk of cutting into your profits with the costs of maintaining redundancy. However, if your operations and supply chain are too lean, then you could face a catastrophe should your supply suddenly be cut off. To meet this goal, you need to consider how to be both lean and redundant. The goal of designing a resilient supply chain can help with that. On the other side of the coin, when it comes to information and data, there's no such thing as too much redundancy. Because maintaining redundant systems, after they're set up, is a relatively low-cost proposition, this part of your goal is more easily met.

- **Designing a resilient supply chain:** The flexibility that a resilient company needs can be found in a resilient supply chain, and that's why this is a very important goal. If you and your team are not certain how to meet this goal, I suggest studying the supply chains of companies that face unpredictable demand, such as fashion retail, electronics and computers. Consider risk pooling, the theory of postponement, interchangeable engineering and collaborating with supply chain partners and customers.[32]

- **Developing your management and staff into inspirational leaders:** Because inspirational leadership is critical to being a bold organization, you should never stop developing inspirational leadership.

---

[32] Yossi Sheffi, *The Resilient Enterprise: Overcoming Vulnerability for Competitive Advantage.* (Cambridge, MA: MIT Press, 2005), pp. 270-279.

## Monitoring the Supply Chain: United Technologies

United Technologies is a global technology corporation. To monitor its extensive supplier network and critical parts, it uses a supplier tracking service. Scott Singer, the director of global supply management at United Technologies, describes the service as "An important tool for us, serving as an early warning system to alert us to possible problems with a supplier so that we can do proactive follow up."

For example, recently the service, which is provided by Open Ratings, Inc., helped a United Technologies aerospace unit identify a supplier with a cash flow problem. Because United Technologies learned of the problem before it had profound effects, they were able to work out a solution.

United Technologies also maintains redundant sources for critical parts. It is Singer's opinion that the biggest risk to the supply chain is two or three levels down in the supplier network. "At a plant level, we define those critical materials that would mandate a secondary source," Singer says. He adds that it is crucial that they do so, despite the fact that finding secondary sources isn't easy."

---

" Doug Bartholomew, "Supply Chains at Risk," *Industry Week*, October 2006, pp. 55–60.

To meet these goals, your plan should include strategies for:
- Governance and compliance
- Emergency communications and management
- Reliability
- Business continuity and resumption
- Information management, protection and recovery
- Business recovery
- Security and safety

Last, but not least, your plan should have a model of success. Let's take a closer look at these strategies and the model of success.

### Governance and Compliance

A business resiliency plan needs a well-managed system of checks and balances that focuses on implementing resiliency goals in a structured and controlled environment. Otherwise, you cannot measure progress and investments against your goals. Therefore, your business resiliency planning team must create a governance and compliance strategy that creates such an environment by defining specific metrics for service delivery, response, availability and other service levels and commitments. These metrics must mesh with your business goals and budgets and must also meet any compliance requirements for a specific industry. The strategy should also define the organizational elements of the plan, quantify the objectives and metrics and set up the program for managing the plan. This includes setting parameters, measuring the work to be performed, tracking progress, analyzing the results and presenting status reports regularly.

### Emergency Communications and Management

During a crisis, a communication breakdown can result in lost lives, lost business and the avoidable consequences of a poor response to an unplanned event. That is why an emergency communications strategy is an important part of a business resiliency plan. Communication with critical information sources (such as first responders, civil authorities, facilities staff and utility providers) sets the stage for properly assessing an incident and its impact. Employee communication allows the flow of vital information to ensure safety, security and the proper response to the crisis. Keeping in contact with clients, business partners and stakeholders is key to preserving the enterprise's reputation and marketability. Communicating with key vendors, outside service providers and other third parties is critical to establishing smooth continuation of business activities.

This strategy should include documented crisis and emergency response plans, because communications and response are top priorities in ensuring the safety of personnel and the viability of operations during and after an emergency. Part of these plans should be a clear definition of who will take the leadership role in the management of the emergency. Inspirational leaders know how to handle emergencies. But it is best to establish a clear leader who will instill confidence and who those involved in the crisis can count on to make sure the right information is communicated to the right person.

*Reliability*

Business resiliency goals cannot be effective without individual strategies that specify how objectives will be achieved. The people and teams in charge of meeting the objectives need feasible, practical and documented strategies in place. Supply chain partners, key service providers and outsourcing providers must participate in this process to be capable of providing an appropriate response during a business interruption or unexpected surge in demand. If you have already included representatives from these partners and providers, then creating this strategy is easier than if you wait to call on them until you are developing and documenting your strategy.

Reliability strategies can call for operational redundancy, or they may simply identify an alternate location from which to operate. In either case, it is critical that strategies, detailed plans, and measures be in place to assure that systems, data and personnel will be available to meet the objectives. Failing to develop and fund effective strategies, as well as failing to empower employees and teams to carry out the plans, can expose you to potentially excessive downtime costs and loss of opportunity.

*Continuity and Resumption*

Sustaining business operations during an unplanned event might require workarounds, alternate workspace or other special arrangements. Therefore, your business resiliency planning team must identify, prioritize and map business processes for all supporting functional requirements, including voice communications, fax, workspace requirements, applications technology and more. They also need to devise and document procedures to account for operational activity between the time an incident occurs and the time when all the recovery activities are complete. These procedures should consider where to go, how to get there and what to do once you get there so that no further confusion occurs during an incident. All these requirements and activities should be documented in a business continuity plan, which must be properly maintained and periodically tested.

*Information Management, Protection and Recovery*

In today's world, a company cannot operate without information and the hardware and software that stores and drives it. Information is the lifeblood of every corporation, and to be competitive, it is critical that companies have information available at all times. Lost information cannot be recovered, and the older the information is, the more difficult it is to re-create. Regulatory agencies such the Department of Health and Human Services, NASD and the U.S. Securities and Exchange Commission have enacted regulations that affect the retention and availability requirements of data for certain businesses. These regulations, coupled with sound business practices, drive the need to protect information under normal working conditions, as well as in the event of a disaster.

Therefore, a business resiliency plan must have a strategy that makes sure that all data is available. This can include offsite backups, mirrored sites, multiplexes and sysplexes—a series of servers set up to operate without interruption should another fail. If the corporate asset known as *data* is not properly protected with a clear, documented strategy, the business can lose revenue and be subject to substantial regulatory fines.

If information is the lifeblood of an organization, technology is the system of vessels and arteries needed to keep it flowing throughout the company. Most IT departments are managed as an internal service to the business. Typically, there are service-level agreements by which users measure these departments. Service must be provided under normal conditions, as well as during emergency or disaster conditions. Business application priorities will dictate the business recovery planning team's technology redundancy, the recovery strategy and the level of investment to be made in the technology resiliency architecture.

Examples of such priorities are the amount of system downtime that can be tolerated from the point of disaster to functional recovery (recovery time objectives, or RTO) and the amount of data loss that can be tolerated during a system recovery (recovery point objectives, or RPO). If your business is totally dependent on technology, a resiliency goal may be set that requires no single-point-of-failure in the support environment. For less technology-dependent businesses, next-day recovery is probably adequate. IT disaster recovery plans, then, should combine service continuity (fail-over) with restoration, accounting for all levels of RTO/RPO specified by the business. The first step of the plan involves the people and tools required to maintain or restore the environment. The next step is the implementation guidebook, which details the order of steps, anticipated timeframes and interdependencies. Without these plans, a technology recovery attempt can result in problems that can negatively affect the ability to recover at all.

*Business Recovery*

Even the most well-prepared organizations and supply chains will experience some sort of business disruption. Therefore, a business resiliency plan must take that possibility into account and contain a documented business recovery strategy. This plan should take into account what will be needed to restart production, how restored supplies will be distributed, how and when infrastructure will be repaired and how and when IT systems will be restored. Some strategies include raising production levels with overtime, suppliers and customer resources.

The issues your recovery plan should focus on are client notification, operations response and IT response. It should create and describe recovery teams, action plans and recovery options. It should also describe who is responsible for the plan, including who holds it and who is responsible for maintenance. The business resiliency planning team must be realistic as it develops this strategy. Depending on the severity of the event and the disruption it has on your facilities, systems and business, recovery could take a significant amount of time.

*Security and Safety*

As we all know, not all business disruptions are caused by natural disasters that destroy distribution networks. Business disruptions can also be caused by people—terrorists, disgruntled workers, labor union strikes and unstable governments. As a result, safety and security is an important business resiliency goal. To address both, your business resiliency planning team should develop a security and safety strategy that:

• Uses layered and balanced defense methods: Layered defense means having several measures in place so you do not rely solely on one method. Having a security guard, a security alarm and video cameras to protect a facility is a simple example. The methods used to protect defense information systems—fail-over, clustering, site mirroring, provisioning—are complex examples. It is important that you balance these methods. You need to know what threat is most likely to harm you the most, and make sure that it has a higher degree of attention than mitigating a risk that is not likely to occur.

• Separates threats from baseline activity: In a large company, you cannot always determine what is a threat and what is normal activity. For example, computer systems generate logs and logs of activity. An inexperienced person looking at those logs might see the word "error" and think there was a problem with the system, when in fact the error is a benign result of a test process. An experienced administrator knows what error messages indicate a true problem. Your security and safety strategy must do the same thing.

- Builds company and supply chain awareness and sensitivity to security and safety: Security is not achieved alone—not for a company or a person. The global companies and supply chains of today mandate a high level of communication, collaboration and awareness both within the walls of a company and outside. Your supply chain partners and your employees all have a role to play in security and safety, and your security strategy must make them aware of that.

- Includes security and safety training and drills: If a company does not experience a threat or disruption for several years, it can become complacent. This is something that your safety and security strategy must address through training, tests, drills, reenactments and renewed company awareness to prevent complacency and keep preparedness levels high.

- Integrates security into business processes: When you wait until after an event to add security measures, or if you try to add them to mature business processes, you get a bandage that hides the wound but which does not go about healing it or preventing another. This is another reason why it is important to have representatives from all parts of your business on the resiliency planning team—they can become advocates and contributors to re-structuring business processes that include security and safety measures.

*Business Resiliency Plan Model of Success*

You cannot have a successful business resiliency plan without ways to determine if it is successful. An important task for any business resiliency planning team is to create a Business Resiliency Model of Success. In my book, *Revolution*, I describe in detail how to create a model of success for your organization.[33] The same principles apply to a business resiliency plan.

A model of success has five parts:

1. Vision: A description of where you are headed
2. Mission: The path for accomplishing the vision
3. Requirements of success: The science of your business
4. Guiding principles: The values you practice as you pursue your vision
5. Evidence of success: Measurable results that will demonstrate when your organization is moving towards the vision

---

[33] Tompkins, *Revolution*, pp. 55-83.

For a business resiliency plan, your planning team addresses resilience in each part. For the vision, they should describe in clear, brief terms their vision of business resilience. Then, they should summarize the business resiliency goals as the mission. For the requirements of success, they should address their strategies for meeting the goals. Next, they should describe the values that the team and the company will practice to pursue the vision. The final step, evidence of success, requires that the team set forth metrics for determining whether the requirements of success are being met.

After the team creates the model of success, the team must make sure your entire company accepts it. It must be instilled in every person in the company and even among your supply chain partners. In doing so, your team will be getting the company to work together as one entity to gain business resilience, because business resilience cannot be achieved by a fragmented, divided company working as separate parts. By working to gain organizational alignment with the Business Resiliency Model of Success your team is taking the next steps in the process of achieving business resiliency—communication, evaluation and reevaluation.

## The Importance of Communication to Successful Business Resilience

Earlier in this chapter, I mentioned that information is the lifeblood of an organization and that technology makes up the vessels and arteries that carry it. Both are extremely important to the health and well-being of a company, but neither is worth as much without communication. Communication is the key to the success of a business resilience plan, because if we don't communicate or communications break down, then there are disastrous consequences from which we might not be able to recover. In plain terms, if you kill the communication within an organization, then you are most likely going to kill the organization along with it.

It is not enough to simply communicate, either. You must communicate properly and to all the right people or your communication efforts will probably be in vain. In other words, you must provide the right communications to all the right people at the right time—just as you want to make sure that the right products and services get to the right customers at the right time. In some ways, communication is to resilience as food is to the body—the right communication promotes health and resilience, and the wrong or incomplete communication can erode health and resilience—and even destroy them.

The communication you need for business resilience must be simultaneous, instantaneous and multi-directional to allow not only your employees but also your supply chain partners to work at the same time rather than sequentially. This can help eliminate unnecessary inventory buffers and accelerate the flow of supplies from one partner to the next. It must also provide a framework for dynamic planning and make strategic information available to all partners so that they can be aware, in real time, of changing customer needs and trends, possible kinks or bottlenecks in the supply chain and global events or policies that might affect the flow of supplies, raw materials, and goods.

The communication between partners, leaders and employees must be relevant, open and honest. All parties must be linked by various means, and you must integrate information requirements into the communications process. What is harder to achieve, but nonetheless is the most critical requirement for communications that promote business resilience, is a willingness to share key information–withholding nothing, regardless of whether the party you are communicating with is down the hall or thousands of miles away in a boardroom that is not yours.

To achieve these kinds of communications, you must eliminate communication silos. I first wrote about this in the twentieth century, but it seems that it is still a problem. For example, communication and information silos are among the issues that are eating at the profitability of banks, as they lose customers to competitors because their separate divisions do not or will not share information. If information is not shared and accessible to all links of the supply chain, then your business resilience plan is going to be in jeopardy. Therefore, your company and its partners must use every means of communication possible for managing and transmitting all types of data and information along the supply chain. In a sense this is like the layers of security I mentioned in the previous section—the more ways you have to send information, the more likely your partners and employees are to receive it. This includes face-to-face and interpersonal communication.

The communication system best suited for business resilience is one that integrates four essential types of capabilities. It must be able to handle day-to-day communications and transactions (both paper and e-commerce) along the supply chain. It must facilitate planning and decision making, support the demand and shipment planning necessary for distributing resources effectively and handle vendor managed inventory programs. It must provide tools like an integrated network model that will allow strategic analysis. And, finally, it must be resilient in itself. When your business resiliency planning team is developing a strategy for information and technology management, protection and recovery, the emphasis should be on reducing the likelihood of communication disruption and working toward quick recovery should major communication systems fail.

## Evaluation and Reevaluation

Evaluating and reevaluating your business resilience plan is made easier by the Business Resiliency Plan Model of Success that your planning team developed. In the Evidence of Success part of the model, your team will have laid out metrics that must be met if business resiliency is to be achieved. Some realistic performance measures you can use to determine how your company and your supply chain are doing are:

- **Robustness:** The strength or the ability of organizational elements and systems to adapt to or withstand given levels of disruption or interruption without suffering degradation, loss of function or performance.
- **Responsiveness:** The ability to anticipate and adapt to disruptions, so stakeholder confidence in your company is maintained.
- **Resourcefulness:** The capacity to identify challenges and opportunities, establish priorities and mobilize resources when conditions exist that could threaten your company's performance.
- **Rapidity:** The capacity to meet performance priorities and achieve goals in a timely fashion so that you contain losses to the lowest levels possible if there is a disruption or even a surge in demand.
- **Redundancy:** The extent to which organizational elements and systems can be substituted to satisfying performance and functional requirements in the event of a disruption.

These are just a few of the many measurements you can evaluate as part of the evidence of success and to make sure that your business resiliency plan is on the right track.

I would like to stress here that it is not enough to evaluate your plan once or twice. In this business world of acceleration and speed, situations are subject to quick and sudden changes. Supply chains are much more fluid than they used to be, and so is business. That is why you must review and rank your operations periodically, as well as update your plans. You should also perform assessments based on the questions listed in the Appendix regularly to make sure that new risks have not arisen. I recommend that your business resiliency planning team determine the number of times a year that they should meet to reassess vulnerabilities, compare company progress, changes in the environment and marketplace, and any shifts in demand. I also recommend that you involve your customers. Ask them how you're doing, and ask them to tell you how you could improve. You should also do this on a regular schedule.

## Work the Plan

A business resiliency plan that is communicated to all the right people at the right time and periodically reviewed is the key to achieving the business resilience that is part of being bold. In these days of lean supply chains and globalization that create greater distances between facilities and supply chain partners while making next-door neighbors of us all, you cannot be resilient without a plan. Yet these supply chains challenge your business resiliency plan, because there are more people to share it with, and it is possible that they don't speak your language. So, developing, communicating, evaluating and reevaluating the plan will not be easy, but like all worthwhile endeavors, the benefits will be immense. When other companies are faced with a handful of bruised apples, you'll be selling applesauce.

# Wal-Mart, Starbucks and a P&O Ports Help Desk: Communication for Business Resilience

The hurricanes that flattened the Gulf Coast in August and September 2005 tested corporate logistics and supply chain operations, as companies struggled to move relief supplies and inventory to and from the region before and after each storm. One lesson from these storms is that having procedures for communicating quickly about what needs to be done is as essential for companies as having integrated inventory and logistics systems.

Wal-Mart, for example, was able to move food, water, generators and other goods to areas hit by hurricanes Katrina and Rita following each storm, because it has an emergency operations center that is staffed every day around the clock by decision-makers who have access to all of the company's systems.

The emergency response team works in a room designed with efficient communication in mind. When a district manager calls from the field to tell the operations manager in the center that he needs 10 trucks of water, the operations manager can turn to the person staffing the replenishment systems. As a result, Wal-Mart trucks were distributing aid to Katrina's victims days before federal relief arrived. Wal-Mart shipped about 3,000 containers of goods to the region.

Starbucks was also able to get aid to hurricane-ravaged areas quickly. When the company got a request from the American Red Cross to donate coffee, managers at headquarters contacted the company's distributors to discuss how they could help. Starbucks determined that it could donate 30,000 pounds of coffee, 235,000 bottle of water and 44,000 pastries without affecting supplies to its retail stores. Efficient communication also helped many companies avoid losing goods in the storm.

In 2003, P&O Ports, North America opened a Help Desk located in North Carolina to help trucking companies and their drivers navigate the real estate and systems of the Napoleon Avenue Container Terminal in New Orleans. After the storm, the Help Desk took on a new role as trucking companies that were still able to operate contacted the Help Desk when they could not reach other call centers and organizations because of the destruction of phone lines and wireless networks. When the Port of New Orleans reopened on September 21, 2005, trucks were able to drive in to pick up containers full of supplies. This was because the Help Desk contacted the trucks that had originally contacted it to let them know the Port was open.[v]

---

[v] Ben Worthen, "How Wal-Mart Beat Feds to New Orleans," *CIO*, 1 Nov. 2005, http://www.cio.com/archive/110105/tl_katrina. html?CID=13532

## On the Elevator

To be resilient and prepare for business interruption and vulnerability, you need a business resiliency plan that can protect and improve your customer satisfaction, brand reputation, people and profits while providing a proactive, comprehensive and robust strategy for achieving and maintaining competitive advantage. It must create a flexible and adaptive underlying operational infrastructure that also protects against the unknown, unexpected threats or challenges. This plan should encompass not only your internal operations, but your external networks and your supply chain.

The process of developing a business resilience plan starts with the creation of a business resiliency planning team. The makeup of this team is critical and should include members from all functional areas in the company, because business vulnerability and resiliency affects everyone. The business resiliency planning team should also reach outside the physical boundaries of your company to include representatives from your suppliers and outsourcing providers. The team should gather the results of your assessments, which is critical information for the formulation of your business resilience plan.

A business resiliency plan should have resiliency goals for ensuring that a company is flexible, adaptable, redundant and secure. These goals include:
• Reducing the possibility of disruptions
• Learning and sharing for safety and security
• Building in redundancies
• Designing a resilient supply chain
• Creating inspirational leaders throughout your organization
To meet these goals, your plan should include strategies for:
• Governance and compliance
• Emergency communications and management
• Reliability
• Business continuity and resumption
• Information management, protection and recovery
• Business recovery
• Security and safety

Your plan should also have a model of success which will help you take the next steps in the process of achieving business resiliency—communication, evaluation and reevaluation. Communication is the key to the success of a business resilience plan, because if we don't communicate or communications break down, then there are disastrous consequences from which we might not recover.

Evaluating and reevaluating your business resilience plan is made easier by the Business Resiliency Plan Model of Success that your business resiliency planning team developed. In the Evidence of Success part of the model, your team will have laid out metrics that must be met if business resiliency is to be achieved. It is not enough to evaluate your plan once or twice: you must review and rank your operations periodically, as well as update your plans. You should also perform assessments based on the questions listed in the Appendix regularly to make sure that new risks and issues have not arisen.

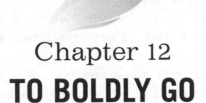

# Chapter 12
# TO BOLDLY GO

"To boldly go where no one has gone before."

– "Star Trek"

When I think about being bold, I often come back to the famous line from "Star Trek," "To boldly go where no one has gone before." In many cases, to maintain competitive advantage and to gain greater market share, a bold company must go where no company has gone before. You need new, creative methods for getting those 15 pounds of apples into that 5-pound bag. Will it be your company that reduces the size or number of apples to fit them into the bag, or will you find someone else to do it? Will you find a company to make you a better bag? And what will you do if suddenly you can't get the apples where they need to be?

Inspirational leadership and the motivated, enthusiastic leaders it creates can help you with the bold answers to these questions. When inspirational leaders are spread throughout your company and at all levels, you will discover that the courage and spirit inherent in these leaders will move them to get extraordinary things done and to make a difference, and your company will be caught up in that action. These fearless leaders, led by an inspirational leader (you), will try all kinds of things with those apples— things that you or a few people alone might not have considered.

Implementing the ideas behind inspirational leadership in your company will equip you for tackling the subject of core competency, and its offshoot, outsourcing. You and your leaders have the tools for taking a long, hard, critical look at your organization to determine if you are focusing on the right processes and activities. They will help you define those functions that truly add value to your company and those that you would be better served having another company do for you. They also will help you face the possibly difficult facts and tasks that come from defining core, as well as outsourcing secondary core or primary non-core functions. Together, you will use the careful evaluation and analysis required to make those decisions.

You will also tap their creativity and innovation, as well as your own, to come up with innovative outsourcing strategies, including making sure that your outsourcing providers are as bold as you are and as prepared as you are for anything. Once that is done, they will be there when your unique method of using the apples reaps the benefits of a lean production system, or when you put your brand on an apple product that a bold manufacturer made for you.

And when your bold company faces an unexpected glitch, such as the loss of a supplier, a critical server crash or a shipping route that is suddenly closed, you and your bold, inspirational leaders and your bold outsourcers will not just find a way around that glitch. You will also use that glitch for competitive advantage by boldly going where your company has not gone before. This is bold business resilience—it goes beyond recovering from an unexpected disruption or disaster. It means thinking of disruptions and even disasters as opportunities to tighten supply chains and increase flexibilities, so you can respond to this world of accelerated pace and change.

Consider this my challenge to you. Dig deep into your inspirational leadership skills to inspire others. Being bold is about taking charge and making something happen. Bold leaders in bold companies do not sit back and wait to see what happens—they take an active role in making good things happen. So, what are you waiting for? Get out there and get moving so that you can boldly take your company where it has not been before. I'm confident that it will be an exciting ride full of opportunity and promise. And the best part is that only good things will follow.

GO!GO!GO!

# Chapter 13
# ON THE ELEVATOR

Business acceleration is affecting all of us. Customers want our products, and they want them now. However, downsizing, reengineering, re-layering and deverticalization have created smaller companies with fewer employees and more complex and diverse supply chains. Therefore, there is no longer enough time in the day, week or even year for us to get everything done quickly. To meet the business challenges created by today's new realities, the place to be professionally is in a bold organization that encourages collective and individual growth. To be bold takes a combination of:

- Inspirational leadership
- Core competency identification
- Business resilience

## Inspirational Leadership

Inspirational leadership is a combination of characteristics that gives people the courage and spirit to move from wherever they are and further their abilities to lead others so that they can get extraordinary things done and make a difference. Inspirational leadership is more than being a leader—it is about inspiring others to lead with a combination of heart, deeds, learning and being, rather than doing.

Inspirational leadership is about tapping the wellsprings of human motivation and about fundamental relationships with your fellow man. It is about setting examples by deeds rather than by words. Inspirational leadership is also about learning while leading, especially in the face of obstacles. Inspirational leadership requires planning, executing, managing and controlling. It also requires constituents, or supporters, who must be enlisted and not commanded. Enlistment comes from dialogue and not monologue.

The good news about inspirational leadership is that you don't have to "wing it." Inspirational leadership involves the following fundamental practices:

159

- Challenge the process: Challenging the process is a fundamental practice of inspirational leadership because being a bold organization means changing the status quo.
- Inspire a shared vision: To act on this practice, imagine a better future for your company. Think big and think positively. Once you have done that, you can't keep it a secret. You need to communicate this future with your constituents enthusiastically and passionately, until they share not only your vision of the future but also your enthusiasm and passion.
- Enable others to act: Leaders use the word "We" to include others. You cannot be an inspirational leader of a bold organization without the help of your constituents.
- Model the way: To be an inspirational leader, you must act the way you want your constituents to act. You must show them your commitment to your shared vision, goals and values.
- Encourage the heart: Inspirational leaders know that heart is an integral part of a bold organization. Encouraging the heart by building self esteem is critical to being an inspirational leader.

Being an inspirational leader means believing that you are a leader, understanding what leaders do, learning, teaching, creating revolutions and motivating. Inspirational leaders prepare their organizations for change, and they constantly challenge the status quo to make things happen.

## Core Competency

Outsourcing is a management tool that shifts the organizational structure of companies. It is a business transformation process that is a key component in the process of becoming a bold organization and can create great opportunity for improved performance. When done properly, outsourcing primary non-core operations functions yields numerous benefits. The key to taking advantage of all outsourcing has to offer lies in your outsourcing strategy—defining your core competencies, defining targets and managing your outsourcing relationships.

The process of defining core requires awareness of the four types of business functions within a company—primary core, secondary core, primary non-core and secondary non-core. Primary core functions are the things that differentiate your company in the marketplace and, more importantly, they are the reason your customers come to you. Secondary core functions bring value to your customer and must be done well, but at the same time are not visible to your customer. Primary non-core functions are those that can affect your relationship with your customer, but are not what your business is about. Secondary non-core functions are those processes that are necessary for running the business, but do not affect your company's success.

To select specific functions for outsourcing, an internal baseline analysis and market research is required for each specific function to determine whether it should be selected or outsourcing. After the baselining and market research initiative is complete, you and our outsourcing team can determine the feasibility of outsourcing specific functions. Then, it is time to solicit providers for the process or processes being outsourced. This is one of the most critical components of the outsourcing process, and it must be done properly. To prepare an RFP that will allow you to select the best provider, you must take the following actions:

- Clearly set forth the goals to be achieved by outsourcing, keeping in mind that your primary goal will be to return leadership and management focus to the levels necessary for peak performance.
- Develop a detailed, realistic timeline for the outsource process.
- Involve senior management early, often, and at key decision points.
- Be certain that a wide range of candidates are pre-qualified before sending the RFP.
- Clearly define the scope of what is to be outsourced.
- Establish a benchmark based on doing the functions to be outsourced yourself.
- Be certain the RFP provides a clear set of requirements, a clear path forward and a clear desire for innovation and creativity.
- Share the outsourcing process and timeline with each qualified provider. Be sure all candidates are given the same information and the opportunity to present their best bid.
- Evaluating proposals and choosing your final candidate is a time-consuming process. A key thing to keep telling yourself is "Success is all in the details."

As you begin the process of building a lasting relationship with your provider, an important thing to remember is that there is no "off the shelf" approach to the relationship. Establishing a relationship that is geared toward long-term success is as much an art as it is a science. To create the right kind of partnership with your outsourcing provider, you and your provider must function as a cohesive, collective whole. Once you have put a continuous improvement process in place, your relationship with your provider has a greater chance of growing, improving and remaining strong. Most outsourcing initiatives are long term, and if you and your provider communicate well and challenge each other, you will be able to take changes and surprises in stride.

## Business Resilience

Business disruptions can do immeasurable harm to a company. They can keep companies from delivering on promised goods and services to their customers, and they can create a domino effect throughout a supply chain. The impact of these disruptions can be drastic, not just in terms of business loss or serious reductions in revenue, but also because they reveal, sometimes internally and sometimes publicly, the vulnerability of business and how much of our supply chains can be out of our control. The good news is that business vulnerability and disruption need not destroy your company or hack holes into your supply chain that takes years to fix. Businesses can mitigate vulnerability or even use the adversity that comes with business disruption to soar past their competitors The secret to doing either of these is business resiliency—the ability to bounce back after a business disruption. The process of achieving business resilience can be broken into five steps:

1. Assess.
2. Plan.
3. Communicate.
4. Evaluate.
5. Re-evaluate.

If your company is populated with inspirational leaders, has embraced the robust outsourcing strategy outlined in the last part of this book, and has an innovative plan for business resiliency, then you can overcome any business disruptions or even use them to your advantage.

# Appendix
# ASSESSING YOUR BUSINESS RESILIENCY

As I stated in Chapter 10, the first step toward achieving business resiliency is to assess (followed by plan, communicate, evaluate and reevaluate). It's important that you understand where your company is in terms of vulnerability, preparation for disruption and resiliency. This means reviewing your company's forecasting and planning, inventory abilities and communication in detail and then extending that review to your supply chain and supply chain partners. Your focus should be identifying gaps and bottlenecks, identifying the areas that are critical to supply chain performance and identifying vulnerability.

Over the years, Tompkins Associates has had clients that needed our help assessing their processes and supply chains with an eye to decreasing vulnerability and building in business resiliency. We have developed a list of questions that organizations can answer, and we weight the questions and their answers based on their impact on the organization's vulnerability and resiliency.

In this appendix, I present these questions in their entirety. You should use them as a solid foundation for assessments that are specific to your company. In other words, these questions are meant to prompt you to develop accurate assessments of your vulnerabilities, which will help you recognize what you must do to achieve bold business resilience.

I start with questions for assessing IT, because a company's daily operations depend heavily on its IT infrastructure. I then share questions about physical security and structure, operations processes and the supply chain. For each assessment, I recommend using a rating system, such as 0 to 10 with 0 being the lowest and 10 being the highest, to answer the questions.

## IT Assessment

It's no secret that IT plays a pivotal role in the success of any company and therefore in a company's resiliency. If a virus strikes your network or a series of workstations, if a key server goes down or if key routers and switchers are disabled by a disaster, it is very difficult to keep your business running. Therefore, assessing your IT infrastructure, software and its connections to your supply chain partners is a very good place to start.

When Tompkins Associates conducts an IT assessment, we look at four sub-areas: personnel, physical, planning and recovery. Some of the questions in the assessment may seem repetitive or redundant, but in reality, they are supposed to be applied differently in the various sub-areas.

### Personnel Sub-Area

Some of the questions to ask about IT personnel are:

- Do you have a current IT organization chart?
  - Do you screen the people who work in the IT department?
  - Do you perform reference checks?
  - Do you verify certifications?
  - Do you perform criminal background checks?
- Do you have a policy for allocating personnel resources across your user base?
  - How are personnel resources allocated across your user base?
  - Do you allocate based on user type?
- Are users required to change passwords on a frequent basis?
- Are all employees instructed on the proper procedures in the event a computer virus is detected on their individual workstations?
- Do you have a system administrator?
- Does your organization provide its own support?
  - Does your organization have a full-time staff of software support?
  - Does your organization have a full-time staff of hardware support?
- In your staffing plan, do you have key employee backups, cross training status, contact lists, phone trees and so on?
- Is in-house expertise on staff to make corrections?
  - Trouble shoot?
  - Repair?
  - MTTR (Mean Time to Repair)?
- Has your network ever been hacked into?
  - How often?
- Does your organization have an established structure in place for approving the access of users to different accounts, systems and applications?
- Are CDs, memory sticks, laptops and other digital storage devices reviewed before being taken from your facility?
- Are e-mail messages scanned?
- Are e-mail attachments reviewed?

### Physical Sub-Area

Some of the questions to ask about the physical IT infrastructure are:

- Is the IT area secure?
  - How do you limit access to your equipment?
  - Do you have fire protection in your computer room? What type?
  - Where are your backup tapes/disks stored, on-site or off-site?
- Does your organization have a set of policies and procedures related to backing up critical data and applications?
  - Are server backups performed on a regular basis?
  - Are backup policies and procedures followed?
  - Are users required to store or backup their data on a server?
  - Are regular user backups verified?
  - Are there resources available to perform the restore procedure?

- Do you have a firewall for your network?
  - Is your firewall internally managed?
  - Has your firewall ever been breached?
- Do you have intrusion detection software?
  - Have you ever had a network security audit?
  - Are event logs maintained and regularly reviewed for discrepancies/potential intrusion attempts?

### Planning Sub-Area

Some of the questions to ask about your IT planning are:

- Do you support multiple locations?
  - Can individual locations work independently of other locations?
- Do you have a network topology map?
  - How many servers do you have?
  - How many operating systems do you support?
  - How many different kinds of systems/applications do you run in your operations? (i.e. WMS, personnel, payroll, purchasing, accounting)
  - Are these applications required to be available 24/7?
  - Do your IT systems link to fire alarms, burglar alarms?
  - How many users do you support at each location?
  - Do you have installation copies of all operating systems?
  - Have you ever had a physical security audit?
  - What type of equipment do you have in the facility? Mainframes, servers, PCs?
  - Is your facility "hard-wired" or do you use RF technology?
- Do you have an uninterruptible power supply (UPS)?
  - How long will the UPS last?
  - Are you on a backup generator?
- Do you know all the single point failures in your system?
  - Do you know the operational impact of these single point failures?
  - Do you have adequate spares or maintenance agreements in place to support your availability requirement?
  - Have you designed redundancy or manual work-around for these single point failures?

○ What is your most critical application? Next? After that, and so on?

○ How long could your business continue without voice communications?

○ How long could your business continue without data communications?

○ How long without both?

○ Could IT provide required operations support if telecommunications services were lost?

• Does your organization maintain any redundant, "hot" failover systems?

• Does your organization have a network security policy?

○ Do you have network policies backed up?

○ Do you have network monitoring tools installed?

• Do you have virus software installed?

○ How often is your virus software updated?

○ How often does a virus intrusion disable a user workstation, server or application?

• Do you have switch and router configurations backed up?

• Do you have a backup "paper-based" system for business transactions?

○ Do you have a documented backup and archive process?

○ How often is data backed up?

○ Do you have "off-site" secure backup repository locations with formalized procedures to ensure that backups are successful?

○ Can operations data be backed up and restored selectively?

• Do you have an IT contingency plan?

○ In the event of a system failure, are there established, documented restore procedures?

○ Are the restore procedures documented, accessible and reviewed regularly?

○ Are there regular, periodic tests of the capabilities of backup systems?

○ Are you staffed to perform repair and maintenance activities, or do you contract them out?

○ Do you have maintenance agreements documenting response times and procedures for critical devices?

○ Do you have an IT strategic plan that you are following?

○ Have you had more than one major failure in your system in a three-month period?

○ Do you know what caused the last major failures?

○ Do you have a means to do failure trend analysis?

○ Do you review failure data on a regular basis?

○ Are those single points of failure protected? By redundant equipment? Ancillary resources? Hot backups? Other protection?

○ What is the probability of failure of one of these components and sub-systems?

○ Have you redesigned parts of your system based on failure data analysis?

○ Do you have a policy to purge old data?

*Recovery Sub-Area*

Some of the questions to ask about your IT recovery are:

• Do you have an active alternate site for rebuilding a computer facility?

• What IT applications would be critical to continue business?

• Do you have process documents/procedures for recovery?

• Do your recovery process documents/procedures cover:

- Server failure?
- Disk failure?
- Switch/hub failure?
- Corrupted files?
- Corrupted programs or program configurations?
- LAN failure/cut or damaged line?
- Backup failures?
- Virus invasions?
- Fire wall breaches?
- Do you have intrusion detection installed and running?
- Do you get meaningful information from the network monitoring tools?
- How often do you change system passwords?
- Does your company create/code enhancements for the systems used in the company?

- Is all of the code reviewed before it is released to the user group?
- Does the IT department review current production code for undocumented changes?
- Do you have a software preventative maintenance plan (for example, data file and database management, backup, etc.)?
- Do you have a hardware preventative maintenance plan?
- Do you keep maintenance logs for your software and hardware?
  - What percent of equipment is at or near end of life?

## Physical Security Assessment

For a physical security assessment, the questions you ask take into consideration three sub-areas: environment/location, operations and human exposures.

### Environment/Location Sub-Area

Because of the global nature of the marketplace, it's possible that your company has numerous facilities located in different regions or on different continents. You should ask these questions about the environment/location of each of your facilities:

- Is your facility located in a flood plain?
  - How have you prepared your facility for flooding?
- Does flash flooding occur in your neighborhood?
  - How have you prepared your facility for flash flooding?
  - If flash flooding is frequent, what are your procedures for handling it?
- Is access to your facility dependent on culverts, overpasses or underpasses subject to flooding?
  - How have you prepared for flooding of the access to your facility?
  - If access to your facility frequently floods, what are your procedures

for handling it?
- Do tornadoes occur in your locale?
  - How have you prepared your facility for them?
  - If tornadoes occur often in your locale, what are your procedures for handling them?
- Is your locale often affected by hurricanes?
  - How have you prepared your facility for them?
- Is there seismic activity in your area?
  - How have you prepared your facility for earthquakes?
- Is your facility subject to severe winter storms?

# IT Sample Answers

At the beginning of this appendix, I mentioned how Tompkins Associates uses a scale of 0–10 to rate the responses to our assessment questions. The way we rate the answers to five of the IT questions is:

- Does your organization have full-time software support?
  - No (0–1)
  - Someone in the office supports software (2–3)
  - Part-time contractor (4–6)
  - Outsource all software support (7–8)
  - We have full-time software support (9–10)
- How do you limit access to your equipment?
  - Not limited (0–3)
  - Secure environment (4–8)
  - Secure environment with passwords (9–10)
- Do you know the operational impact of single point failures?
  - Don't know (0–2)
  - Some of the impact (3–5)
  - Most of the impact (6–9)
  - Yes (10)
- In the event of a system failure, are there established, documented restore procedures?
  - No (0–2)
  - We've talked about them (3–4)
  - There are procedures but not current (5–6)
  - There is updated documentation but it is not tested (7–8)
  - All documentation is current and tested (9–10)
- Do you get meaningful information from network monitoring tools?
  - We have no network monitoring tools (0–4)
  - Network is monitored externally (5–9)
  - Network is monitored internally and externally (10)

○ How have you prepared your facility for severe winter storms?

○ If your facility is frequently subject to severe winter storms, what are your procedures for handling them?

• Is there an airport within 20 miles of your facility?

○ Is your facility located in an airport approach or takeoff corridor?

• Is your facility near a waterway, highway or railroad where hazardous materials are transported?

○ How have you prepared your facility for possible releases of toxic chemicals?

*perations Sub-Area*

Some of the questions you should ask about the operations in each of your facilities are:

• Does a neighboring facility use hazardous materials which may pose explosion or toxic release hazards?

○ How have you prepared your facility for possible explosions or releases of toxic chemicals?

• Is your facility more than 20 years old?

○ Do you have a structural inspection and maintenance program?

○ Do you have an electrical inspection and maintenance program?

• Do you have an electrical substation?

○ Where is your substation located?

○ How is the substation protected?

• Do you have main electrical switchgear?

○ Where is your switchgear located?

○ How is the switchgear protected?

• Is the source of your drinkable water an on-site well?

○ How is the well head protected?

• Do you have a municipal source of drinkable water?

○ Where is the main control valve?

• Is the source of your non-drinkable water an on-site well?

○ How is the well head protected?

• Do you have a municipal source of non-drinkable water?

○ Where is the main control valve?

• Does your facility use natural gas?

○ Where is your natural gas main located?

○ How is the control valve protected?

• Is there a possibility of a fire occurring in your facility?

○ What is the planned response to a fire in your facility?

○ Do you have fire sprinkler protection in your facility?

○ Is it a "control" or a "suppression" system?

○ Is there a fire company which provides coverage in your area?

○ How close to your facility is the nearest fire company?

○ Is there a railroad crossing between your facility and the nearest fire company?

• Do you have hazardous materials in your facility?

○ Are these materials in separate, secured areas?

○ What would be your response to a release or incident involving these materials?

○ Do you have highly hazardous chemicals that exceed OSHA Process Safety Management thresholds?

○ Do you use flammable liquids or gases in your process?

○ Are these materials present in any one location in excess of 10,000 pounds?

• Do you use any type of gases in your process?

○ Are these gases compressed?

• Is welding, burning, or cutting performed in your facility?
  ◦ Is a hot work permit system in place?

• Are you concerned that your level of emergency/disaster planning might be inadequate?
  ◦ How do you describe your level of planning?

*Human Exposures Sub-Area*

Some of the questions to ask about human exposures at your facility or facilities are

• Are you concerned about access to your facility and operations?
  ◦ Is your facility fenced?
  ◦ How is entry to your facility controlled?
  ◦ How is access controlled inside your facility?
  ◦ Do you have closed circuit television to monitor facility access and employee common areas?
• Is labor a key resource in your facility?
  ◦ How would you rate the relationship between your management team and your workforce?
  ◦ Is there an established grievance policy or procedure?
  ◦ How often is the grievance procedure used?
• Are various skills required to conduct operations?

  ◦ How would you rate the skills of the majority of your workforce?
  ◦ What is the availability of potential workers in your locality that have the correct skill sets for your business?
  ◦ Do members of your management team have designated "seconds" to perform functions in their absence
• Do you use "temporary" workers provided by an agency?
  ◦ Does the temporary agency perform background checks?
• Does your employment application ask for prior work experience and references?
  ◦ Do you follow up with background and reference checks before hire?

## Operations Assessment

When Tompkins Associates conducts an operations assessment, we look at five sub-areas: management, machines, materials, personnel and operational planning. These sub-areas are further divided into categories that vary, depending on the sub-area. These categories are outlined below.

Common to the management, machines, materials and personnel sub-areas are the manufacturing and maintenance categories. The management, materials and personnel sub-areas also have procurement and distribution categories.

The operational planning sub-area has these nine categories: forecasting, customer purchasing, raw materials and finished goods inventory management, inventory control dependent item demand calculation, production scheduling, management and information technology, network configuration and receiving and stocking.

*Management Sub-area*

Procurement

Some of the questions you should ask in the procurement category for the management sub-area are:

- How is procurement managed?
- What performance parameters are measured and reported?
- To what extent are individual employees autonomous in daily activities?
- To what extent are natural work teams cohesive and able to create change?
- Do you have detailed, written documentation of your procurement process(es)?
    - Is the documentation updated regularly?
    - Is it clear where each process starts and finishes and how it interacts with other processes?
    - Are all current procurement needs recognized and understood?
    - Are procurement manuals and other documentation stored in a central location and easily accessible?
    - Is the procurement process documentation stored in a central location and easily accessible?
    - Is responsibility clearly defined for each of your procurement processes?
- Have you identified impediments (lack of alternate sources, lack of pricing and delivery information, lack of demand forecasts, etc.) to your procurement process(es)?
    - To what extent can you dissolve the impediments?
    - To what extent have you carried out those improvements?
- Do you measure procurement performance (e.g., on-time inbound deliveries, vendor fill rates, etc.)?
    - To what extent have mitigating actions been identified and implemented?

- For each of your vendors, have you identified the critical points of failure for their performance?
    - Do you know the acceptable limits your procurement processes must meet to be effective?
    - Have you identified which steps are critical to be completed in a particular way, at a particular time or at a particular level of skill or authority, etc.?
    - Have you done a failure modes effect analysis to identify mission-critical procurement activities?
    - Do you have vendor parameters that signal impending breakdowns in the procurement process?
- Are there historical records of vendor performance?
- If vendor reliability is not known explicitly, can you determine it from procurement records?
- Do you have defined safety stock levels?
- How are safety stock levels determined?
- How often are safety stock levels updated?
- Do you have contingency plans in place for critical elements of your procurement process?
- Are those contingency plans documented?
- Can you identify contingency sources of sub-contractor services (e.g., painting, galvanizing, heat-treating, etc.)?
- Can you identify alternate sources for raw materials and purchased services?
- Have prior arrangements been completed such that the contingency plans can be implemented rapidly?
- Have possible alternate procurement scheduling techniques (expedited raw materials, sub-contractors, etc.) been identified?

- Have prior arrangements been completed such that alternate scheduling can be implemented rapidly?
- Have you identified non-critical procurement that could be deferred if necessary?
- Have you determined when deferral becomes critical?
- If procurement can be deferred, is the necessary pre-work completed?

- Have you identified mitigating actions for procurement decision-making (cross-training, alternate communications, etc.) should they become necessary?
- Have the identified mitigating actions for procurement decision-making been implemented?

## Manufacturing

Some of the questions you should ask in the manufacturing category for the management sub-area are:

- How is manufacturing managed?
- What performance parameters are measured and reported?
- To what extent are individual employees autonomous in daily activities?
- To what extent are natural work teams cohesive and able to create change?
- Do you have detailed, written documentation of your manufacturing process(es)?
  - Is the documentation updated regularly?
  - Is it clear where each process starts and finishes and how it interacts with other processes?
  - To what extent are all current manufacturing needs recognized and understood?
  - Are operating manuals and other documentation stored in a central location and easily accessible?
  - Is the documentation of the manufacturing processes stored in a central location and easily accessible?
  - Is responsibility clearly defined for each of your manufacturing processes?
- Have you identified impediments (lack of raw materials, drawings, tooling, machine availability, etc.) to your manufacturing process(es)?
  - To what extent can you dissolve the impediments?

- To what extent have you carried out those improvements?
- Do you measure manufacturing performance (e.g. error-free critical steps, cycle time, specific outcomes, etc.)?
- Have the risk factors for key manufacturing decision-making and scheduling been identified?
- To what extent have mitigating actions been identified and implemented?
- For each of your manufacturing processes, have you identified the critical points of failure for that process?
  - Do you know the tolerances your maintenance processes must meet to be effective?
  - Have you identified which steps are critical to be completed in a particular way, at a particular time or at a particular level of skill or authority, etc.?
  - Have you done a failure modes effect analysis to identify mission-critical manufacturing activities?
  - Do you have parameters that would signal impending customer service problems if manufacturing is not performed?
- Are there historical records of the manufacturing processes used and their success rates?

- If manufacturing process reliability is not known explicitly, can you determine it from manufacturing records?
- Do you have contingency plans in place for critical elements of your manufacturing process?
- Are those contingency plans documented?
- Can you identify contingency sources of manufacturing capability?
- Can you identify alternate sources for other services (laboratory, uniforms, contract packaging, environmental testing, waste disposal)?
- Have prior arrangements been completed such that the contingency plans can be implemented rapidly?
- Have possible alternate manufacturing scheduling techniques (reassignment to other lines, increased lot sizes, alternate sequencing, etc.) been identified?
- Have prior arrangements been completed such that alternate scheduling can be implemented rapidly?

- Have you identified non-critical manufacturing operations that could be deferred if necessary?
  - Have you determined when deferral becomes critical?
  - If manufacturing can be deferred, is the necessary pre-work completed?
- Have you identified mitigating actions for manufacturing decision-making (cross-training, alternate communications, etc.) should they become necessary?
  - Have the identified mitigating actions for alternate manufacturing decision-making been implemented?

## Maintenance

Some of the questions you should ask in the maintenance category for the management sub-area are:

- How is maintenance managed?
- What performance parameters are measured and reported?
- To what extent are individual employees autonomous in daily activities?
- To what extent are natural work teams cohesive and able to create change?
- Do you have detailed, written documentation of your maintenance process(es)?
  - Is the documentation updated regularly?
  - Is it clear where each process starts and finishes and how it interacts with other processes?
  - To what extent are all current maintenance needs recognized and understood?
  - Do you have complete documentation for all internal control systems for automated equipment?
  - Are maintenance manuals and other documentation stored in a central location and easily accessible?
  - Is the documentation on the maintenance processes stored in a central location and easily accessible?
  - Is responsibility clearly defined for each of your maintenance processes?
- Have you identified impediments (lack of access, inadequate training, no spare parts, lack of tools) to your maintenance process(es)?
  - To what extent can you dissolve the impediments?
  - To what extent have you carried out those improvements?
  - Do you measure maintenance performance (e.g., error-free critical steps, cycle time, specific outcomes, etc.)?

- Have the risk factors for key maintenance decision-making and scheduling been identified?
- To what extent have mitigating actions been identified and implemented?
- For each of your machines, have you identified the critical points of failure for that machine's operation?
  - Do you know the tolerances your maintenance processes must meet to be effective?
  - Have you identified which steps are critical to be completed in a particular way, at a particular time, or at a particular level of skill or authority, etc.?
  - Have you done a failure modes effect analysis to identify mission-critical maintenance activities?
  - Do you have machine parameters that signal impending breakdowns if maintenance is not performed?
- Are there historical records of the business processes (downtime / failures, etc.) and the maintenance processes?
  - If equipment reliability is not known explicitly, can you determine it from maintenance records?
- Do you have preventive maintenance (PM) programs in place?
  - Do the PM procedures conform to the manufacturer's recommendations for procedure and frequency?
  - Do you maintain service agreements for all critical pieces of equipment?

- Do those agreements provide standards for expected response times?
- Do you have contingency plans in place for critical elements of your maintenance process?
  - Are those contingency plans documented?
  - Can you identify contingency sources of maintenance services?
  - Can you identify alternate sources for spare parts?
  - Have prior arrangements been completed such that the contingency plans can be implemented rapidly?
  - Have possible alternate maintenance scheduling techniques (expedited parts, subcontractors, etc.) been identified?
  - Have prior arrangements been completed such that alternate scheduling can be implemented rapidly?
- Have you identified non-critical maintenance that could be deferred if necessary?
  - Have you determined when deferral becomes critical?
  - If maintenance can be deferred, is the necessary pre-work completed?
- Have you identified mitigating actions for maintenance decision-making (cross-training, alternate communications, etc.) should they become necessary?
  - Have the identified mitigating actions for alternate maintenance decision-making been implemented?

## Distribution

Some of the questions you should ask in the distribution category for the management sub-area are:

- How is distribution managed?
- What performance parameters are measured and reported?
- To what extent are individual employees autonomous in daily activities?

- To what extent are natural work teams cohesive and able to create change?
- Do you have detailed, written documentation of your distribution process(es)?

- Is the documentation updated regularly?
- Is it clear where each process starts and finishes and how it interacts with other processes?
- To what extent are all current distribution needs recognized and understood?
- Do you have complete documentation for all systems for automated equipment and software (e.g., WMS, TMS, pick-to-light)?
- Are operating manuals and other documentation stored in a central location and easily accessible?
- Is the documentation of the distribution processes stored in a central location and easily accessible?
- Is responsibility clearly defined for each of your distribution processes?

- Have you identified impediments (e.g., inadequate inventory, order processing delays, lack of a locator system, insufficient pallets or totes) to your distribution process(es)?
  - To what extent can you dissolve the impediments?
  - To what extent have you carried out those improvements?
  - Do you measure distribution performance (e.g. order accuracy, on-time shipments)?
- Have the risk factors for key distribution decision-making and scheduling been identified?
  - To what extent have mitigating actions been identified and implemented?
- For each of your distribution processes, have you identified the critical points of failure for that process's operation?
  - Do you know the tolerances your maintenance processes must meet to be effective?
  - Have you identified which steps

are critical to be completed in a particular way, at a particular time, or at a particular level of skill or authority, etc.?
- Have you done a failure modes effect analysis to identify mission-critical distribution activities?
- Do you have parameters that signal impending breakdowns in distribution processes?

- Is the reliability of the distribution processes explicitly known?
  - If distribution process reliability is not known explicitly, can you determine it from distribution records?
- Do you have contingency plans in place for critical elements of your distribution process?
  - Are those contingency plans documented?
  - Can you identify contingency sources of distribution services?
  - Have prior arrangements been completed such that the contingency plans can be implemented rapidly?
  - Have possible alternate distribution scheduling techniques (split shifts, merge-in-transit, partial shipments, air freight, etc.) been identified?
  - Have prior arrangements been completed such that alternate scheduling can be implemented rapidly?
- Are there non-critical distribution operations that could be deferred if necessary (rewarehousing, etc.)?
  - Have you determined when deferral becomes critical?
  - If distribution can be deferred, is the necessary pre-work completed?
- Have you identified mitigating actions for distribution decision-making (cross-training, alternate communications, etc.) should it become necessary?
  - Have the identified mitigating actions for alternate distribution decision-making been implemented?

*Machines Sub-area*

Manufacturing

Some of the questions you should ask in the manufacturing category for the machines sub-area are:

- Does your operation manufacture products?
- Are machines used in your product manufacturing operations?
- What types of machines are used in your operation?
- How many of each do you have?
- Which product types use each of the different types of machines?
- What types of machines are used in your operation?
- How many of each do you have?
- Which product types use each of the different types of machines?
- Does your operation use compressed air?
  - Do you have a single, central air compressor station?
  - How large is the main compressor?
  - Does your operation have a spare air compressor?
  - How large is the spare compressor compared to the main air compressor?
  - How is the spare compressor installed?
  - How much total air compression capability do you have in excess of normal demand?
  - To what extent is your operation dependent on compressed air?
- Does your operation use steam or superheated water?
- How much total boiler capacity do you have in excess of normal demand?
  - To what extent is your operation dependent on steam or superheated water?
  - Does your operation require overhead cranes and hoists?
  - How much excess lift capacity and capability do you have in excess of normal demand?
- To what extent is your operation on overhead cranes and hoists?
- Does your operation use electricity at voltage(s) different from the utility transformer secondary?
  - To what extent do you have excess transformer capacity?
  - To what extent is your operation dependent on electricity at voltage(s) different from the utility transformer secondary?
- Does your operation use cooled, chilled or refrigerated air?
  - Do you have a single, central chiller or refrigeration system?
  - How much total air cooling, chilling or refrigeration capability do you have in excess of normal demand?
  - To what extent is your operation dependent on cooled, chilled or refrigerated air?
- How large is the main system?
  - Does your operation have a spare system?
  - How large is the spare system compared to the main system?
  - How is the spare system installed?
- Does your operation have a water well?
  - To what extent do you have excess well water?
  - To what extent is your operation dependent on well water?
- Does your operation have an ion exchange or similar water treatment system?
  - To what extent do you have excess water treating capacity?
  - To what extent is your operation dependent on water which you treat?
- Does your operation require LPG, propane or butane?

- To what extent do you have excess LPG, propane or butane storage capacity?
- To what extent is your operation dependent on LPG, propane, or butane?
- Does your operation generate electricity for internal consumption?
  - To what extent do you have excess electrical generation capacity?
  - To what extent is your operation dependent on the electricity that you generate?
- Does manufacturing operate approximately 40, 80, 120 or 160 hours per week?

- Is there any technical reason why additional shifts could not be scheduled if personnel were available?
  - To what extent has pre-planning been completed for additional personnel and/or additional shifts?
  - With your current operating shifts, approximately how much manufacturing capacity do you have in excess of normal demand?
  - How difficult would it be to expand manufacturing capacity with the current number of shifts?

## Maintenance

Some of the questions you should ask in the maintenance category for the machines sub-area are:

- What types of machines do you have in your maintenance shops?
- What crafts do you use in this facility (pipefitter, millwright, electrician, instrument, carpenter, insulator, painter, etc.)
  - Which crafts are employed and which are contracted?
- Does maintenance operate approximately 40, 80, 120 or 160 hours per week?
- Is there any technical reason why additional shifts could not be scheduled if personnel were available?

- To what extent has pre-planning been completed for additional personnel and/or additional shifts?
- With your current operating shifts, approximately how much maintenance capacity do you have in excess of normal demand?
  - How difficult would it be to expand maintenance capacity with the current number of shifts?

## Materials Sub-area

### Procurement

Some of the questions you should ask in the procurement category for the materials sub-area are:

- Do you purchase raw materials?
  - What types of raw materials do you purchase?
  - Approximately how much do you purchase every year?
- Who are your major suppliers?
  - How long have you been purchasing raw materials from them?

- What's the nature of your relationship with them?
- Do you get ASNs from them?
- How long have you been purchasing raw materials from them?
- Do you have visibility to their inventory?

- ○ Do you collaborate on production scheduling?
- ○ Approximately how large is the raw materials inventory?
- Are any of the raw materials you purchase customized or engineered specialty products (as opposed to commodities)?
  - ○ Are there unique specifications developed for purchased raw materials?
  - ○ How are unique specifications checked prior to release to the supplier?
  - ○ Are there unique drawings for purchased raw materials?
  - ○ How are unique drawings checked prior to release to the supplier?
- Are there standard specifications for purchased raw materials?
  - ○ How comprehensive are the standard raw material specifications?
  - ○ How meaningful are the standard raw material specifications?
  - ○ How current are the standard raw material specifications?
  - ○ Are standard raw materials specifications revised and re-issued?
  - ○ How are standard raw material specification revisions handled?
- Are there standard drawings for purchased raw materials?
  - ○ How comprehensive, meaningful and current are the standard raw material drawings?
  - ○ Are standard raw materials drawings revised and re-issued?
  - ○ How are standard raw material drawing revisions handled?
- How rigorous is your raw material inspection program?
  - ○ What percentage of raw materials SKUs is inspected?
  - ○ What process is used for assessing the results of the inspections?
  - ○ Who completes the inspection?

- ○ Do you have a vendor certification program which negates the need for inspection of raw materials on receipt?
- ○ Are raw materials rejected based on product quality issues?
- Are raw materials with known quality issues received (as opposed to being returned to the vendor)?
  - ○ How are raw materials that are received with quality issues handled?
  - ○ What has to occur to allow the raw materials with quality issues to be used for production?
  - ○ How are rejected raw materials stored?
  - ○ Who has access to the rejected raw materials storage area?
- Are your vendors notified of product quality issues?
  - ○ Is there a mutually established failure rate or similar product quality goal?
  - ○ How is the inspection data presented to the supplier?
  - ○ Do you or the vendor seek to identify root causes for raw material failures?
  - ○ Is there an action plan for addressing the root causes?
  - ○ How regularly is the action plan monitored and progress reviewed?
  - ○ Are the root causes identified, addressed and resolved?
  - ○ How are raw material suppliers rewarded for exceptional quality?
- Are any of the raw materials chemicals, bio-actives, explosives, poisons or similar agents?
  - ○ Are legal requirements for handling exceeded?
  - ○ Are legal requirements for the employees' right-to-know exceeded?
  - ○ Are legal requirements for storage exceeded?

- Can raw materials be tracked prior to being consumed in production?
- Can raw materials be tracked after being consumed in production?

- How are you notified if you have received products being recalled by the supplier?

## Manufacturing

Some of the questions you should ask in the manufacturing category for the materials sub-area are:

- What types of product inspection processes do you have (visual, dimensional, physical—mechanical or electrical, chemical, etc.)?
  - When is inspection performed (after set-up and before initiation of production, after production, etc.)?
  - What percent of production is inspected?
  - Who performs the inspection?
  - Is the inspection done in-line, beside the line, or off-line?
- Do you manufacture products?
- Are any of the products you manufacture customized or engineered specialty products (as opposed to standard products)?
  - Are there unique specifications developed for manufactured product?
  - How are unique specifications checked prior to release to production?
- Are there unique drawings for manufactured product?
  - How are unique drawings checked prior to release to production?
- Are there standard specifications for manufactured product?
  - How comprehensive are the standard product specifications?
  - How meaningful are the standard product specifications?
  - How current are the standard product specifications?
  - Are standard product specifications revised and re-issued?
  - How are standard product specification revisions handled?

- Are there standard drawings for manufactured products?
  - How comprehensive are the standard product drawings?
  - How meaningful are the standard product drawings?
  - How current are the standard product drawings?
  - Are standard product drawings revised and re-issued?
  - How are standard product drawing revisions handled?
- How rigorous is your product inspection program?
  - What percentage of products is inspected?
  - Are products inspected at multiple stages during the manufacturing process?
  - What process is used for assessing the results of the product inspections?
  - Who completes the product inspections?
- Is product rejected based on quality issues?
  - How is rejected product stored?
  - Who has access to the rejected product storage area?
- How are products with quality issues handled?
  - Is product with known quality issues processed further (as opposed to being reworked)?
  - What has to occur to allow products with quality issues to be used for production?
- Who is notified of product quality issues?

- Is there a failure rate or similar product quality goal?
- How is the inspection data presented to management?
- Do you seek to identify root causes for off-specification product?
    - Are the root causes identified, addressed, and resolved?
    - Is there an action plan for addressing the root causes?
    - How regularly is the action plan monitored and progress reviewed?
- How are production personnel rewarded for exceptional quality?
- Are any of the manufactured products chemicals, bio-actives, explosives, poisons or similar agents?
    - Are nuclear elements used in your manufacturing process?
    - Are legal requirements for handling hazardous materials exceeded?
    - Are legal requirements for the employees' right-to-know about hazardous materials exceeded?
    - Are legal requirements for storage exceeded?
    - Are legal requirements for nuclear equipment inspections exceeded?
- Can work-in-process product be tracked prior to being consumed in production?
- Can work-in-process product be tracked after being consumed in production?

## Maintenance

Some of the questions you should ask in the maintenance category for the materials sub-area are:

- Do you purchase all of the common types of spare parts/MRO items?
- What types of spare parts/MRO inspection processes do you have (visual, dimensional, physical - mechanical or electrical, chemical, etc.)
- Approximately how large is the spare parts/MRO inventory?
- Do you purchase spare parts or consumable maintenance, repair and operating supplies (MRO)?
    - Are any of the spare parts/MRO items you purchase customized or engineered specialty products (as opposed to commodities)?
- Are there unique specifications developed for purchased spare parts/MRO items?
    - How are unique specifications checked prior to release to the supplier?
- Are there unique drawings for purchased spare parts/MRO items?
    - How are unique drawings checked prior to release to the supplier?
- Are there standard specifications for purchased spare parts/MRO items?
    - How comprehensive are the standard spare part/MRO item specifications?
    - How meaningful are the standard spare part/MRO item specifications?
    - How current are the standard spare parts/MRO items specifications?
    - Are standard spare part/MRO item specifications revised and re-issued?
    - How are standard spare part/MRO item specification revisions handled?
- Are there standard drawings for purchased spare parts/MRO items?
    - How comprehensive are the standard spare part/MRO item drawings?
    - How meaningful are the standard spare part/MRO item drawings?
    - How current are the standard spare part/MRO item drawings?
    - Are standard spare part/MRO item drawings revised and re-issued?
    - How are standard spare part/MRO item drawing revisions handled?

• How rigorous is your spare part/MRO item inspection program?
  ○ What percentage of spare part/ MRO SKUs is inspected?
  ○ What process is used for assessing the results of the inspections?
  ○ Who completes the inspection?
  ○ Do you have a vendor certification program that negates the need for inspection of spare parts/MRO items on receipt?
  ○ Are spare parts/MRO items rejected based on product quality issues?
  ○ Are spare parts/MRO items with known quality issues received (as opposed to being returned to the vendor)?
  ○ How are spare parts/MRO items that are received with quality issues handled?
  ○ What has to occur to allow the spare parts/MRO items with quality issues to be used for equipment maintenance?
  ○ How are rejected spare parts/MRO items stored?
  ○ Who has access to the rejected spare parts/MRO items storage area?
• Is the vendor notified of product quality issues?
  ○ Is there a mutually established failure rate or similar product quality goal?
  ○ How is the inspection data presented to the supplier?

○ Do you or the vendor seek to identify root causes for spare part/MRO item failures?
○ Is there an action plan for addressing the root causes?
○ How regularly is the action plan monitored and progress reviewed?
○ Are the root causes identified, addressed and resolved?
• How are spare parts/MRO items suppliers rewarded for exceptional quality?
• Are any of the MRO items chemicals, bio-actives, explosives, poisons or similar agents?
  ○ Are legal requirements for handling exceeded?
  ○ Are legal requirements for the employees' right-to-know exceeded?
  ○ Are legal requirements for storage exceeded?
• Can spare parts/MRO items be tracked prior to being used for maintenance?
• Can spare parts/MRO items be tracked after being used for equipment maintenance?
• How are you notified if you have received spare parts/MRO items being recalled by the supplier?
• How many years old are your spare parts?
• Are electronic spare parts protected from static build-up?
• Are mechanical spare parts protected from moisture?

## Distribution

Some of the questions you should ask in the distribution category for the materials sub-area are:

• Do you purchase shipping supplies (pallets, corrugated cases, tape, labels, returnable containers, stretch/shrink film, dunnage, etc.)?
• Are any of the shipping supplies you purchase customized or engineered specialty products (as opposed to commodities)?

• Are there unique specifications developed for purchased shipping supplies?
  ○ How are unique specifications checked prior to release to the supplier?
• Are there unique drawings for purchased shipping supplies?

- How are unique drawings checked prior to release to the supplier?
- Are there standard specifications for shipping supplies?
  - How comprehensive are the standard specifications for shipping supplies?
  - How meaningful are the standard specifications for shipping supplies?
  - How current are the standard specifications for shipping supplies?
  - Are standard specifications for shipping supplies revised and re-issued?
  - How are standard specification revisions handled for shipping supplies?
- Are there standard drawings for shipping supplies?
  - How comprehensive are the standard drawings for shipping supplies?
  - How meaningful are the standard drawings for shipping supplies?
  - How current are the standard drawings for shipping supplies?
  - Are standard drawings for shipping supplies revised and re-issued?
  - How are standard drawing revisions handled for shipping supplies?
- How rigorous is your shipping supply inspection program?
  - What percentage of shipping supplies do you inspect?
  - What process is used for assessing the results of the inspections?
  - Who completes the inspection?
- Do you have a vendor certification program that negates the need for inspection of shipping supplies on receipt?
  - Are shipping supplies rejected based on product quality issues?
  - Are shipping supplies with known quality issues received (as opposed to being returned to the vendor)?
  - How are shipping supplies that are received with quality issues handled?
  - What has to occur to allow the shipping supplies with quality issues to subsequently be used?
  - How are rejected shipping supplies stored?
  - Who has access to the rejected shipping supplies storage area?
- Is the vendor notified of product quality issues?
  - Is there a mutually established failure rate or similar product quality goal?
  - How is the inspection data presented to the supplier?
  - Do you or the vendor seek to identify root causes for shipping supplies failures?
  - Is there an action plan for addressing the root causes?
  - How regularly is the action plan monitored and progress reviewed?
  - Are the root causes identified, addressed and resolved?
- How are shipping supply suppliers rewarded for exceptional quality?

*Personnel Sub-Area*

Procurement

Some of the questions you should ask in the procurement category for the personnel sub-area are:

- How are your procurement personnel organized?
    - On which shifts do they work?
    - Approximately how much vacation does each get?
- In general, how would you characterize the education and training of your procurement personnel?
- Is there a heavy reliance on a limited number of individuals who know procurement the best?
    - How much of your information resides only with a limited number of individuals?
- Is an individual responsible for review and improvement of your procurement process(es)?
- How do you train your procurement workforce to do their jobs?
- What is the availability of potential additional procurement personnel in your locale?
- Does your procurement management team have designated "seconds" to perform functions in their absence?
- Are your procurement personnel familiar with special issues for hazardous materials?

Manufacturing

Some of the questions you should ask in the manufacturing category for the personnel sub-area are:

- How are your manufacturing personnel organized?
    - On which shifts do they work?
    - Approximately how much vacation does each get?
- In general, how would you characterize their manufacturing education and training?
- Would you rate your manufacturing labor force as skilled?
- Is there a heavy reliance on a limited number of individuals who know your manufacturing processes the best?
    - How much of your manufacturing information resides only with a limited number of individuals?
- Is an individual responsible for each operation in your manufacturing process (at both operational and accountability levels if different)?
- Is an individual responsible for review and improvement of your manufacturing process(es)?
- How do you train your manufacturing workforce to do their jobs?
- Are your manufacturing personnel cross trained?
- Do you use job rotation?
- What is the availability of potential additional manufacturing personnel in your locale?
- Does your manufacturing management team have designated "seconds" to perform functions in their absence?
- Are your manufacturing personnel familiar with special issues for hazardous materials?
- Do you have comprehensive manufacturing safety policies?
    - Are the safety policies disseminated and well understood?
    - Are the safety policies enforced?
    - Is there a functioning safety team?
- Are there documented procedures for executing the manufacturing processes in case of sickness, injury or special circumstances?

## Maintenance

Some of the questions you should ask in the maintenance category for the personnel sub-area are:

- How are your maintenance personnel organized?
  - On which shifts do they work?
  - Approximately how much vacation does each get?
- In general, how would you characterize their education and training?
- Would you rate your maintenance labor force as skilled?
- Is there a heavy reliance on a limited number of individuals who know the maintenance process the best?
  - How much of your information resides only with a limited number of individuals?
- Is an individual responsible for each operation in your maintenance process (at both operational and accountability levels if different)?
- Is an individual responsible for review and improvement of your maintenance process(es)?
- How do you train your maintenance workforce to do their jobs?
- Are your maintenance personnel cross trained?
- Do you use job rotation?
- What is the availability of potential additional maintenance personnel in your locale?
- Does your maintenance management team have designated "seconds" to perform functions in their absence?
- Are your maintenance personnel familiar with special issues for hazardous materials?
- Do you have comprehensive maintenance safety policies?
  - Are the safety policies disseminated and well understood?
  - Are the safety policies enforced?
  - Is there a functioning maintenance safety team?
- Are there documented procedures for executing the maintenance processes in case of sickness, injury or special circumstances?

## Distribution

Some of the questions you should ask in the distribution category for the personnel sub-area are:

- How are your distribution personnel organized?
  - On which shifts do they work?
- Approximately how much vacation does each get?
  - In general, how would you characterize their education and training?
- Is there a heavy reliance on a limited number of individuals who know your distribution processes the best?
- How much of your information resides only with a limited number of individuals?
- Is an individual responsible for each operation in your distribution processes (at both operational and accountability levels if different)?
- Is an individual responsible for review and improvement of your distribution process(es)?
- How do you train your distribution workforce to do their jobs?
- Are your distribution personnel cross trained?
- Do you use job rotation?
- What is the availability of potential additional distribution personnel in your locality?
- Does your distribution management

team have designated "seconds" to perform functions in their absence?

- Are your distribution personnel familiar with special issues for hazardous materials?
- Do you have comprehensive distribution safety policies?
  - Are the safety policies disseminated and well understood?

- Are the safety policies enforced?
- Is there a functioning safety team?
- Are there documented procedures for executing the distribution processes in case of sickness, injury or special circumstances?

*Operational Planning Sub-Area*

Forecasting

Some questions to ask in the forecasting category of the operational planning sub-area are:

- Do your customers provide long range forecasts and share them with you regularly?
  - How do you rate the level and detail of their forecasting?
  - Do you provide feedback to your customers on the accuracy of their sales forecasts for your products?
- Are your forecasting processes formalized and executed in the same manner by each entity?
- Are there frequent interactions between your customers' personnel and your supply chain management personnel (above and beyond contact between your sales personnel and your customers' purchasing personnel)?
  - How do you rate these interactions?

- Is your forecasting of routine demand done with software designed to minimize error?
  - Do your forecasting practices use estimates of sales for one-time events to supplement routine demand to create an overall sales forecast?
  - Is event planning an integral part of your forecasting process?
  - How do you rate your forecasting processes?
- Do you measure and report the accuracy of your sales forecasts against your goals?
  - How accurate are your forecasts?
  - How do you rate your forecasting process?

Customer Purchasing

Some questions to ask in the customer purchasing category of the operational planning sub-area are:

- Do your customers transmit POs to you electronically?
- Do your customers define short range requirements in the form of blanket orders to the maximum extent?
- Do you acknowledge customers' POs and commit to ship dates via Advance Shipping Notices (ASNs)?

- Do you commit to ship dates for products not currently in finished goods inventory?
- Do you use your sales forecasts in calculating finished goods inventory levels?

## Raw Materials and Finished Goods Inventory Management

Some questions to ask in the raw materials and finished goods inventory management category of the operational planning sub-area are:

- Do you know the cost of carrying inventory?
  - Do you use this knowledge in management decisions impacting inventories?
  - How do you rate your understanding and use of inventory carrying cost in decision making?
- Do you know the costs of production line changeover for all your products?
  - Do you use the costs of production line changeover when calculating production run quantities?
  - Do you have an ongoing program for reducing production line changeover time and cost?
- Do you know vendor lead times and are they up to date (accurate)?
- Are SKUs ranked by priority of on-time shipment and divided into classes for the purposes of customer service?
  - Are desired customer service levels defined for each class?
  - Is demand variability calculated dynamically?
- Is safety stock calculated based on the desired level of customer service?
  - Do you take forecast accuracy into account when setting safety stock levels?
- Do you take supplier fill rate and lead time variability into account in setting raw material safety stock levels?
  - Are suppliers' production schedules shared with you and incorporated into your safety stock planning?

## Inventory Control

Some questions to ask in the inventory control category of the operational planning sub-area are:

- Do you maintain inventory buffers to cover interruptions in service?
- Do you measure inventory performance?
- Do you maintain perpetual balances on all significant inventories?
- Do you use cycle counting to maximize the timeliness and accuracy of inventory records?
  - Do you use a strategy for determining how often to count specific SKUs based on their unit price, inventory value, volume, or another economics-based parameter?
- Do you attempt to reconcile some, but not all, differences, based on the amount of the required adjustment?
- Do you have clearly defined policies on by whom and under what circumstances perpetual inventory balances can be adjusted?
- Do you measure and report inventory record accuracy on a gross or absolute basis against your goals?
  - Are your bills of materials complete and up to date?

## Dependent Item Demand Calculation

Some questions to ask in the dependent item demand calculation category of the operational planning sub-area are:

- Is your Manufacturing Master Scheduling being done with an integrated system focused on effective execution?
    - How do you rate your Manufacturing Master Scheduling?
- Do you know your internal lead times?

- Do you calculate quantities of dependent demand items from the sales forecast using Material Requirements Planning (MRP) software?
- Is your Sales and Operations Planning process fully matured and being used to construct production schedules?
    - How do you rate your Sales and Operations planning process?

## Production Scheduling

Some questions to ask in the production scheduling category of the operational planning sub-area are:

- Are your production schedules robust?
- Do you have formal rules by which production schedule change requests are addressed?
- Do you measure production schedule conformance?
- Are there frequent interactions between suppliers' and customers' operations planning personnel and your supply chain management personnel?

- How do you rate these interactions?
- Is Distribution Requirements Planning (DRP) replacing your traditional single-location forecasting practices for multiple tier networks (SKUs stocked in DCs fed by other DCs)?
- How do you rate your evolution to dynamic planning techniques?

## Management and Information Technology

Some questions to ask in the management and information technology category of the operational planning sub-area are:

- Are your planning processes effective throughout the pipeline?
- Do they fully address global supply chain requirements?
- How do you rate the effectiveness of global planning?
- Have your manufacturing planning and execution systems been designed to support the continuous flow of materials and products?
- How do you rate the ability of your manufacturing to support continuous flow manufacturing?

- Is planning done to balance the rate of output of each step in the supply chain so that inventory is minimized?
- How do you rate the balancing steps in your supply chain so that inventory buffers are not required?
- Are simplified pull processes in place to signal the need for material deliveries?
- How do you rate your implementation of lean, pull processes?

# Sample Operations Planning Sub-Area Benchmark Assessment

If you prefer, you can turn your list of questions about each sub-area of an assessment into a benchmark assessment. The table below is an example of a benchmark assessment Tompkins Associates created for a client's operations planning sub-area.

| ITEM # | BENCHMARK ITEM | BENCHMARKING CRITERIA | RATING |
|---|---|---|---|
| | Forecasting | Level and detail of forecasting provided by customers rated as: Excellent—10, Very Good—9, Good—8, Average—7, Below Average—6, Poor—5 | |
| | Your customers provide long range forecasts and share them with you regularly. | | |
| | You provide feedback to your customers on the accuracy of their sales forecasts for your products. | | |
| | Your forecasting processes are formalized and executed in the same manner by each entity. | | |
| | There are frequent interactions between your customers' personnel and your supply chain management personnel (above and beyond contact between your sales personnel and your customers' purchasing personnel). | Rated as: Excellent—10, Very Good—9, Good—8, Average—7, Below Average—6, Poor—5 | |
| | Your forecasting of routine demand is done with software designed to minimize error. | | |
| | Your forecasting practices use estimates of sales for one-time events to supplement routine demand to create an overall sales forecast. | Event planning is an integral part of the forecasting process and is rated as: Excellent—10, Very Good—9, Good—8, Average—7, Below Average—6, Poor—5 | |
| | You measure and report the accuracy of your sales forecasts against your goals. | | |
| | Your sales forecasts are accurate. | The accuracy of forecasting process is rated as: Excellent—10, Very Good—9, Good—8, Average—7, Below Average—6, Poor—5 | |
| | Customer Purchasing | | |
| | Your customers transmit POs to you electronically. | | |
| | Your customers define short range requirements in the form of blanket orders to the maximum extent. | | |
| | You acknowledge customers' POs and commit to ship dates via Advance Shipping Notices (ASNs). | | |
| | You commit to ship dates for products not currently in finished goods inventory. | | |
| | You use your sales forecasts in calculating finished goods inventory levels. | | |

| EM # | BENCHMARK ITEM | BENCHMARKING CRITERIA | RATING |
|---|---|---|---|
| | **Raw Materials and Finished Goods Inventory Management** | Understanding and use of inventory carrying cost in decision making is rated as: Excellent—10, Very Good—9, Good—8, Average—7, Below Average—6, Poor—5 | |
| | The cost of carrying inventory is known and used in management decisions impacting inventories. | | |
| | The costs of production line changeover are known for all your products. | | |
| | The costs of production line changeover are used in calculating production run quantities. | | |
| | You have an ongoing program for reducing production line changeover time and cost. | | |
| | Vendor lead times are known and are up to date, i.e., accurate. | | |
| | SKUs are ranked by priority of on-time shipment and divided into classes for the purposes of customer service. | | |
| | Desired customer service levels are defined for each class. | | |
| | Demand variability is calculated on a dynamic basis. | | |
| | Safety stock is calculated based on the desired level of customer service. | | |
| | You take forecast accuracy into account in setting safety stock levels. | | |
| | You take supplier fill rate and lead time variability into account in setting raw material safety stock levels. | | |
| | Supplier's production schedules are shared with you and incorporated into your safety stock planning. | | |
| | **Inventory Control** | Rated as: Excellent—10, Very Good—9, Good—8, Average—7, Below Average—6, Poor—5 | |
| | Adequate inventory buffers are maintained to cover interruptions in service. | | |
| | You measure inventory performance. | | |
| | You maintain perpetual balances on all significant inventories. | | |
| | You use cycle counting to maximize the timeliness and accuracy of inventory records. | | |
| | You use a strategy for determining how often to count specific SKUs based on their unit price, inventory value, volume or other economics-based parameter. | | |
| | You attempt to reconcile some, but not all, differences, based on the amount of the required adjustment. | | |
| | You have clearly defined policies on by whom and under what circumstances perpetual inventory balances can be adjusted. | | |

| ITEM # | BENCHMARK ITEM | BENCHMARKING CRITERIA | RATING |
|---|---|---|---|
| | You measure and report inventory record accuracy on a gross or absolute basis against your goals. | | |
| | Your bills of materials are complete and up to date. | | |
| | **Dependent Item Demand Calculation** | Rated as: Excellent—10, Very Good—9, Good—8, Average—7, Below Average—6, Poor—5 |  |
| | Manufacturing Master Scheduling is being done with an integrated system focused on effective execution. | | |
| | Your internal lead times are known. | | |
| | You calculate quantities of dependent demand items from the sales forecast using Material Requirements Planning (MRP) software. | | |
| | The Sales and Operations Planning process is fully matured and being used to construct production schedules. | Rated as: Excellent—10, Very Good—9, Good—8, Average—7, Below Average—6, Poor—5 | |
| | **Production Scheduling** | | |
| | Your production schedules are robust. | | |
| | You have formal rules by which production schedule change requests are addressed. | | |
| | You measure production schedule conformance. | | |
| | Distribution Requirements Planning (DRP) is replacing your traditional single-location forecasting practices for multiple tier networks (SKUs stocked in DCs fed by other DCs). | The evolution to dynamic planning techniques is rated as: Excellent—10, Very Good—9, Good—8, Average—7, Below Average—6, Poor—5 | |
| | There are frequent interactions between suppliers' and customers' operations plan personnel and your supply chain management personnel. | Rated as: Excellent—10, Very Good—9, Good—8, Average—7, Below Average—6, Poor—5 | |
| | **Management and Information Technology** | The effectiveness of global planning is rated as: Excellent—10, Very Good—9, Good—8, Average—7, Below Average—6, Poor—5 | |
| | Planning processes are effective throughout the pipeline and fully address global supply chain requirements. | | |
| | Manufacturing planning and execution systems have been designed to support the continuous flow of materials and products. | Manufacturing systems' ability to support continuous flow manufacturing is rated as: Excellent—10, Very Good—9, Good—8, Average—7, Below Average—6, Poor—5 | |
| | Planning is done to balance the rate of output of each step in the supply chain so that inventory is minimized. | Balancing steps in the supply chain so inventory buffers are not required is rated as: Excellent—10, Very Good—9, Good—8, Average—7, Below Average—6, Poor—5 | |
| | Simplified pull processes are in place to signal the need for material deliveries. | Implementation of lean, pull processes is rated as: Excellent—10, Very Good—9, Good—8, Average—7, Below Average—6, Poor—5 | |

| ITEM # | BENCHMARK ITEM | BENCHMARKING CRITERIA | RATING |
|---|---|---|---|
| | **Network Configuration** | Distribution network strategy is rated as: Excellent—10, Very Good—9, Good—8, Average—7, Below Average—6, Poor—5 | |
| | The distribution network has been analyzed, rationalized and revised over the last five years. | | |
| | You have considered, evaluated and determined the proper role of third party logistics over the last five years. | 3PL strategy is rated as: Excellent—10, Very Good—9, Good—8, Average—7, Below Average—6, Poor—5 | |
| | **Receiving and Stocking** | | |
| | You receive Advance Shipping Notices (ASNs) from suppliers on all shipments. | | |
| | You provide feedback to vendors on lead time conformance and fill rate performance. | | |
| | You post receipts of raw materials within eight hours of carrier arrival. | | |

## Network Configuration

Some questions to ask in the network configuration category of the operational planning sub-area are:

- Has your distribution network been analyzed, rationalized, and revised over the last five years?
- How do you rate your distribution network strategy?

- Have you considered, evaluated and determined the proper role of third party logistics over the last five years?
- How do you rate your 3PL strategy?

## Receiving and Stocking

Some questions to ask in the receiving and stocking category of the operational planning sub-area are:

- Do you receive Advance Shipping Notices (ASNs) from suppliers on all shipments?

- Do you provide feedback to vendors on lead time conformance and fill rate performance?
- Do you post receipts of raw materials within eight hours of carrier arrival?

## Supply Chain Assessment

In Chapter 10, I stressed the impact that today's supply chains have on a company's vulnerability and business resilience. Therefore, you cannot assess your company's resilience without assessing your supply chain. This is also a test of your relationships with your supply chain partners: The more you know and communicate honestly with them, the more likely you are to achieve a comprehensive assessment and, in the long run, a stronger and more resilient supply chain.

For our supply chain assessments, we divide the chain into these sub-areas: *suppliers, clients* (if you're a supplier), *systems, lead time, operations, customer visibility, third party operations, change, peak to peak, total operations, customer satisfaction, manufacturing synthesis, distribution synthesis, partnerships* and *communications.*

The questions in this section are very high level and are intended to be a guide to get you started in your assessment. I recommend adding the questions from the operational planning sub-area of your operations assessment to this list, because the answers to those questions require knowledge of your supply chain and your partners.

### *Suppliers Sub-Area*

Some of the questions to ask about your suppliers are:

- Do you have multiple suppliers?
  - Do all suppliers provide equal quality and consistency?
- Do you have international suppliers?

  - Are any of your raw materials or products sourced outside the US?
- Are any suppliers in areas prone to natural disruption—earthquake, flood, etc.?

- What is the maximum/minimum capacity of each supplier?
- Do your suppliers operate their own truck fleets?
- Do your suppliers have redundant shipping options?
- Do you have redundant suppliers for packaging? Supplies?
- Have you reviewed your sourcing for your raw materials or products from your supplier in the past year?
  - Have you performed an analysis of these raw materials or products for alternate sources in the past year?
- Are your raw materials or products delivered just in time?
- How long can you sustain your operations based on your inventory of raw materials or products?
  - Would changing suppliers change lead-times?
- How do you make payments to your suppliers? EDI or Check?
  - Do you have alternate ways to make supplier payments?
- Are your supplier contracts multi-year?

- Have you reviewed your supplier contracts in the past year?
- Have you reviewed your supplier financials in the past year?
- Do you assess quality of your supplier?
  - Do you have a rating system for your suppliers?
  - How is the quality assessment done? On the supplier site? At receiving? None?
  - Do you keep a figure of merit on each supplier?
  - Do you use supplier figure of merit to increase or decrease your management of them?
  - Do you use supplier figure of merit to negotiate contracts with them?
- Are your suppliers subject to union work stoppage?
  - Are your suppliers' transportation networks subject to union work stoppage?
- Do your suppliers have any other customers (governments, certain industries) that might make the suppliers targets for disruption?

## Clients Sub-Area

Some of the questions to ask about your clients if you are a supplier are:

- Do your clients keep supplier statistics?
  - Do you have access to those statistics?
  - Do you review these statistics on a regular basis?
- How long are your contracts with your clients?
- Does your client have alternate sources for your product?
- Have you done a competitive analysis in the past year?
- Do you know your competition?
- Do you feel if you had a high rating in business resiliency it would give you a competitive edge?
- How does your client make payments to you? EDI? Check?

  - Do you have alternate ways of receiving payments?
  - Do you have statistics on accounts receivable?
- Do you do a financial analysis of your clients?
- Is any one of your clients more than 50 percent of your business?
- Do you own your shipping or contract?
- Is your transportation network subject to union work stoppage?
- Do you have alternate means of shipping product?
- How long can you sustain your operations if one of your clients shuts down or could not make payments?

## Systems Sub-Area

Some of the questions to ask about your supply chain systems are:

- Are raw materials and supplies ordered manually or systematically?
  - If ordered by your computer system, are contingency plans up to date?
- Do you have an automated manufacturing system?
- Have your manufacturing planning and execution systems been designed to support the continuous flow of materials and products?

- How do you rate the ability of your manufacturing to support continuous flow manufacturing?
- Do you transmit POs to suppliers electronically?
- Do you receive Advance Shipping Notices (ASNs) from suppliers on all shipments?

## Lead Time Sub-Area

Some of the questions to ask about lead times are:

- Is there an expiration date on material?
- What is lead time?
- If raw material and supplies are equal in quality and prices among vendors, is time in transit and freight cost an issue?

- If so, are you minimizing your on hand inventory by using some of your suppliers in a just-in-time mode?

## Operations Sub-Area

Some of the questions to ask about operations are:

- Are you managing your distribution facilities to the point where they meet all of your metrics?
  - Are your metrics current and considered world-class?

- How long can you operate without delivery of raw materials?
- Could your process accommodate alternative materials?
- If so, are procedures in place to make that change if it is necessary?

## Customer Visibility Sub-Area

Some questions to ask about customer visibility are:

- Do your customers have enough visibility within your systems to have lookup capability to order status, inventory status, back and substitution status?

- Do your customers have visibility to your fleet movements to track their orders?

*Third Party Operations Sub-Area*

Some questions to ask about third party operations are:

- Are there any third party manufacturing or logistics operations?
  - If so, are they audited on a continuous basis?
- Are gain sharing measures initiated to provide a win-win situation if the third party lowers costs?
- Are penalties involved if the third party does not perform as contracted?
- Are the third party facilities practicing security measures consistent with your company (physical, data, employee)?

*Change Sub-Area*

Some questions to ask about the change sub-area are:

- Does each employee have a clearly defined responsibility, accountability, role and identity?
- Has personnel continuity been planned for and are individuals prepared to act?
- Who is responsible for executing contingency plans?
- Do contingency plans prepare individuals to handle additional change within the plan?

*Peak-to-Peak Sub-Area*

Some questions to ask about peak-to-peak are:

- What contingency plans exist to avoid the downturns?
  - Where and by whom will they be executed?
- What problems have already been planned for?

*Total Operations Sub-Area*

Some questions to ask about total operations are:

- Do workflows for each operation exist?
  - Are they current?
  - Who maintains them?
- Where are possible buffers located?
- What alternate methods, resources and processes are possible?

*Customer Satisfaction Sub-Area*

Some questions to ask about customer satisfaction are:

- What are your customers' lead time boundaries?
- What are your customers' quality boundaries?
- What competitors are available to service customer requirements?
- Are any customers integrated with the supply chain?

*Manufacturing Synthesis Sub-Area*

Some questions to ask about manufacturing synthesis are:

- Do you have multiple facilities? How many? Where?
- What are your current lead time requirements?
- What are your current setup times for each product?
- What routings are required currently to make each product?
- What operations are outsourced?
  - What are the capacities and locations of outsourced operations?
- Do WIP buffers exist today?
- What internal operations are available and what are their capacities?
- At what percent capacity do you run manufacturing?
- Do you have redundant sources of power?
- Do you use water, air, refrigeration in the manufacturing process? Redundancy?
- Do you maintain spare parts for manufacturing machinery? Redundancy?
  - What effect would they have on the manufacturing process if out of service?
- What would it cost to have a machine down for a day?
- Is there one critical material the lack of which can stop production?
  - What safety stock of that critical material do you maintain?

- What safety stocks do you maintain of secondary and tertiary materials?
  - Could you accumulate safety stock if necessary?
  - Does your safety stock require specialized storage (refrigeration, heating, humidity control, etc.)?
- Do you have single or multiple lines for your manufacturing process?
- How much, if any, redundant equipment do you maintain for each process step?
- Do you have alternative or backup infrastructure for your process (water, power, gas, air, etc.)?
  - What is the expected duration of alternative/backup infrastructure?
- Do you have a plan for alternative actions (maintenance, replacement, etc.) during interruptions?
  - Do you maintain safety stocks of WIP?
  - Do you maintain an inventory of finished product?
  - Can portions of your operation continue if one or more others are interrupted?
- Is your manufacturing operation unionized?
  - If so, what is the term of the current contract?

*Distribution Synthesis Sub-Area*

Some questions to ask about distribution synthesis are:

- How is raw material transported? Train? Truck? Ship?
- How many carriers do you use?
  - Can you use alternate carriers?
  - How quickly?
- Can you change modes?
  - How quickly?

- Are there alternate routes for the modes you use?
- Are your carriers unionized?
  - If so, how long are their current contracts?
- Can predictable natural events interrupt shipping?

- How much downstream inventory do you have?
- Do you have distribution centers/distributors?
- How long can you go without shipping before customers are affected?
- Are there plans for your customers to find alternate supplies?
- Do you ship across international borders?
- Are your shipments regulated by state, federal or international authorities?
- How much of your outbound transportation network can you control?
- How often do you ship (hourly, several times a day, daily, every other day, weekly)?

- How far do you ship (locally, statewide, regionally, nationally, same hemisphere, globally)?
- What is the average size of a shipment? Weight? Quantity?
- Are there restrictions on incoming raw material? Size? Weight? Height?
- Do you have a Distribution Strategic Master Plan?
    - Is it current?
    - Who maintains it?
    - Are third party logistics providers included?
- What is the basis for current distribution network topology?
    - Is forecasting used to plan product flow through the network?

## Partnerships Sub-Area

Some questions to ask about partnerships are:

- Who are your supply chain member contacts (operational, technical, etc)?
- Is the total pipeline composed of supply chain members?
- What is your basis for selecting an organization as a supply chain member?

- Do you have backup supply chain members?
    - Are backup supply chain member capabilities tested regularly?
- Is supply chain member performance benchmarked?

## Communications Sub-Area

Some questions to ask about communications are:

- What supply chain members do you share information with?
- What products do you use to conduct electronic communications?
- What systems do supply chain members use?

- What transactions are used between supply chain members?
- What transactions are vital to the supply chain?
- What security methods protect the path and content of messages between supply chain members?

## On the Elevator

The first step toward achieving business resiliency is to assess. This means reviewing your company's forecasting and planning, inventory abilities and communication in detail and then extending that review to your supply chain and supply chain partners. Your focus should be on identifying gaps and bottlenecks, areas that are critical to supply chain performance and vulnerability.

Over the years, Tompkins Associates has developed a list of questions that organizations can answer, and we weight the questions and their answers based on their impact on the organization's vulnerability and resiliency.

When Tompkins Associates conducts an IT assessment, we look at four sub-areas: personnel, physical, planning and recovery. For a physical security assessment, the questions you ask take into consideration three sub-areas: environment/location, operations and human exposures.

When Tompkins Associates conducts an operations assessment, we look at five sub-areas: management, machines, materials, personnel and operational planning. These sub-areas are further divided into categories that depend on the sub-area.

Common to the management, machines, materials and personnel sub-areas are the manufacturing and maintenance categories. The management, materials and personnel sub-areas also have procurement and distribution categories.

The operational planning sub-area has these categories: forecasting, customer purchasing, raw materials and finished goods inventory management, inventory control, dependent item demand calculation, production scheduling, management and information technology, network configuration and receiving and stocking.

For our supply chain assessments, we divide the chain into these sub-areas: suppliers, clients, systems, lead time, operations, customer visibility, third party operations, change, peak to peak, total operations, customer satisfaction, manufacturing synthesis, distribution synthesis, partnerships and communications.

# Index